Voices from Primary Sources: American History

Unit 4: Test Practice with Document-Based Questions

Introduction ···

For many students, history is a boring slog through the past. They have to read lifeless renditions of events, and they have to memorize dates and places. Indeed, some historical dates and places are utterly important. Unfortunately, this typical approach to history overlooks the fact that we are all a part of history on a daily basis—and sometimes what we witness becomes historically important. Primary sources are often eyewitness accounts of historical events. These accounts can make history come alive for the student.

This book balances a generous number of primary sources with secondary sources such as charts, graphs, time lines, and historical perspectives by more modern writers. It will help students improve their reading comprehension and social studies skills. The book is excellent practice for the increased use of document-based questions (DBQs) on major tests.

Document-Based Questions (DBQs)

DBQs are an important part of today's educational environment. To understand their world better, students must be able to analyze information as well as the documents that contain that information. Studying and analyzing each group of documents will allow students to develop their critical-thinking skills. Increasingly, social studies exams are using DBQs to assess competence in writing and social studies. This book is designed to help students succeed at answering document-based questions and essays.

Organization

The book uses a scaffolded process to acquaint the student with DBQs.

- **Unit 1: Understanding Basic Documents** introduces the most common types of documents used in testing. Student responses to exercise questions are factual.

- **Unit 2: Finding the Voice** provides more detailed steps to using documents. Student responses to exercise questions are factual and critical.

- **Unit 3: Listening on Your Own** gives students more extensive practice with documents. After studying tip boxes, students examine documents on their own. Student responses to exercise questions are factual and critical. This unit also includes a practice DBQ test and a sample top score essay.

- **Unit 4: Test Practice with DBQs** includes seven practice tests with various documents.

- Other features include an essay scoring rubric and an answer key.

- Beginning on page 118 are five worksheets that you can distribute to students to help them work with different kinds of documents.

Standards

One basic standard of social studies is that students use various intellectual skills to show their understanding of major ideas, eras, themes, and turning points in the history of the United States. To demonstrate this understanding, students should:

- use primary and secondary records to analyze major events that shaped the United States as a nation;

- appreciate historical events through the experiences of those who were present;

- explore American culture by identifying the key ideas, beliefs, and traditions that help define the nation and unite all Americans;

- explain the significance of historical evidence; judge the importance and reliability of evidence; and understand the importance of changing interpretations of history.

Additional Lessons
Using Primary Sources

Two government Web sites, the Library of Congress and the National Archives and Records Administration, provide extensive resources for teachers and students. Both Web sites provide lesson plans for using primary documents in the study of United States history. You can visit these two Web sites at the links below.

Library of Congress:
http://memory.loc.gov/learn/lessons/primary.html

National Archives and Records Administration:
http://www.archives.gov/education/

Features ·······························

Unit 1 introduces the most common types of documents used in testing.

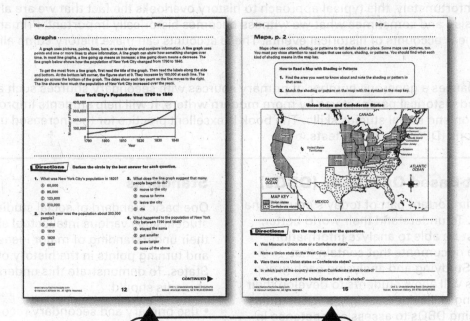

> Student responses to exercise questions in this unit are factual.

> Parts of the document are highlighted to aid student understanding.

Unit 2 gives more detailed steps to using documents.

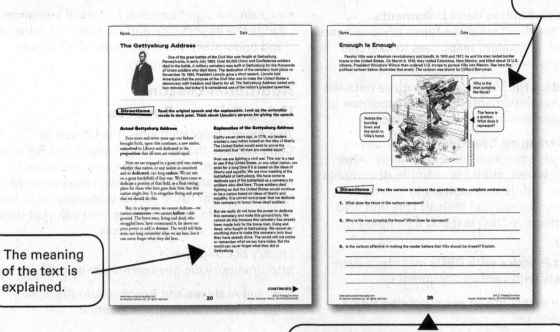

> The meaning of the text is explained.

> Student responses to exercise questions in this unit are factual and critical.

Unit 3 gives students more extensive practice with documents.

A tip box gives students hints on how to approach the document.

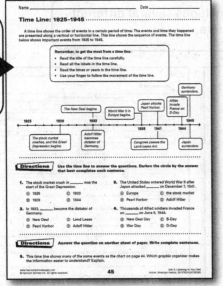

A credit line tells the source of the document.

Captions tell more about graphic images.

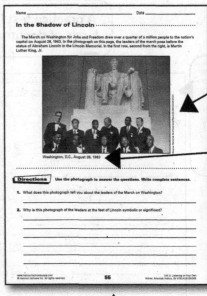

Student responses to exercise questions in this unit are factual and critical.

A practice test gives students a chance to deal with the testing situation without pressure.

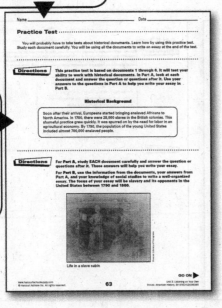

A brief historical background gives students a foundation to understand the documents.

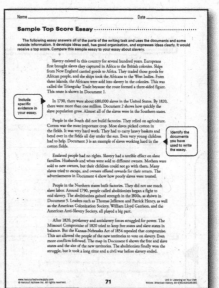

A sample essay shows students what is expected in a well-written essay.

Unit 4 includes seven practice tests with various documents.

A practice test includes several different kinds of documents.

Brief background information is given for many documents.

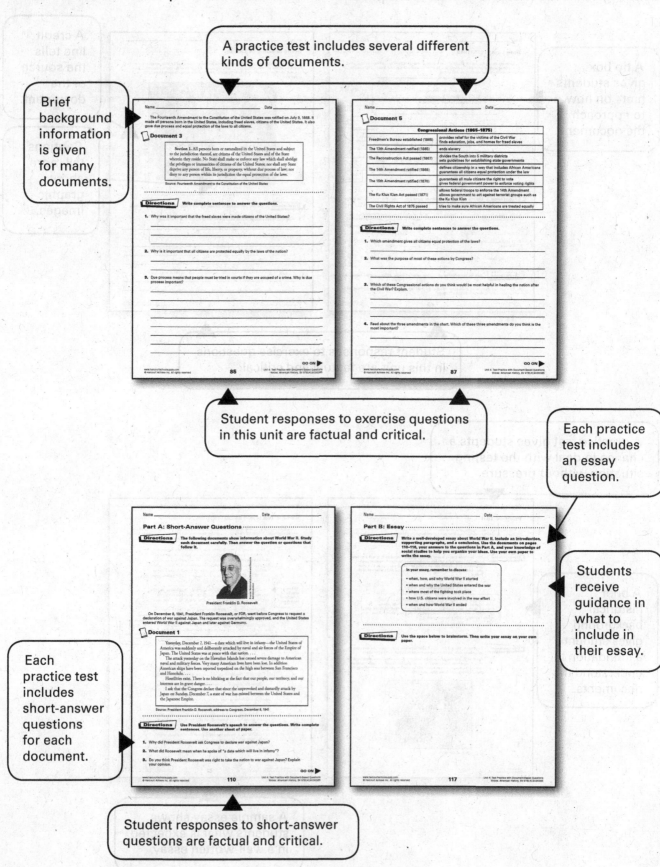

Student responses to exercise questions in this unit are factual and critical.

Each practice test includes an essay question.

Students receive guidance in what to include in their essay.

Each practice test includes short-answer questions for each document.

Student responses to short-answer questions are factual and critical.

Rubric for Document-Based Essays ·······································

	Score of 5	Score of 4	Score of 3	Score of 2	Score of 1	Score of 0
Task	Answers ALL parts of the task	Answers MOST of the task	Answers the task	Answers SOME of the task	Has very little under-standing of the task	Does not answer the task
Documents	Uses the documents and outside information	Uses MOST of the documents and outside information	Uses SOME of the documents and outside information	Uses SOME of the documents and no outside information	Does not clearly use documents and only hints at them	Does not use any documents or hint at them at all
Data	Uses data accurately ALL of the time	Uses data accurately MOST of the time	Uses data accurately SOME of the time	Uses data that is not always relevant	Uses data that is rarely relevant	Uses data that is irrelevant or does not use data
Development	Develops ideas completely	Develops ideas very well	Develops ideas well	Develops ideas poorly	Attempts to develop ideas, but does not	Makes no attempt to develop ideas
Evidence	Uses much supporting evidence	Uses a good amount of supporting evidence	Uses supporting evidence	Uses SOME supporting evidence	Uses very little supporting evidence	Uses no supporting evidence
Organization	Has very good organization and strong development	Has good organization and good development	Has STRONG general plan of organization	Has WEAK general plan of organization	Has no plan of organization	Is unable to be read; illegible
Expression	Always expresses ideas clearly	Expresses ideas clearly MOST of the time	Expresses ideas clearly in general	Expresses ideas clearly SOME of the time	Attempts to express ideas clearly, but does not do so well	Words are confused and illegible

Scoring Rubric
Voices: American History, SV 9781419036385

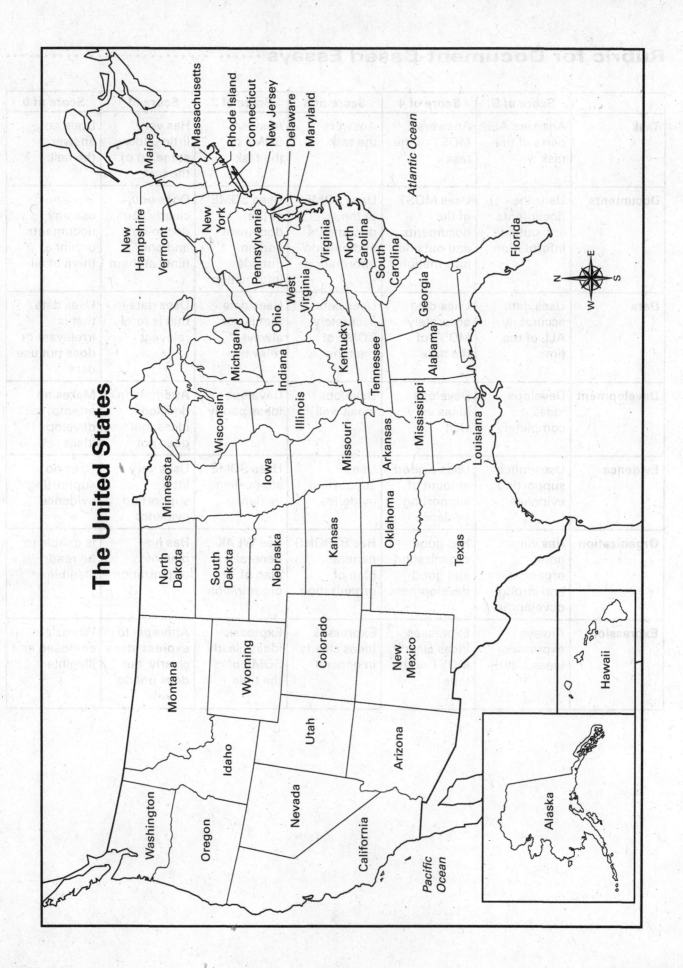

The United States

Maine
New Hampshire
Vermont
Massachusetts
Rhode Island
Connecticut
New York
New Jersey
Pennsylvania
Delaware
Maryland
West Virginia
Virginia
North Carolina
South Carolina
Ohio
Kentucky
Tennessee
Georgia
Alabama
Florida
Michigan
Indiana
Illinois
Wisconsin
Missouri
Arkansas
Mississippi
Louisiana
Minnesota
Iowa
Oklahoma
Texas
North Dakota
South Dakota
Nebraska
Kansas
Colorado
New Mexico
Montana
Wyoming
Utah
Arizona
Idaho
Nevada
Washington
Oregon
California

Atlantic Ocean

Pacific Ocean

Hawaii

Alaska

N E W S

Map of United States
Voices: American History, SV 9781419036385

Name _____   Date _____

Text ··

Much American history you learn will be in written form. You must read the **text** carefully to be sure you understand the meaning. You can't just glance at the words and hope to know what they mean. If you don't understand a word, you should look it up in a dictionary.

Here's a famous piece of writing from American history. It is called the Preamble to the Constitution of the United States.

We the People of the United States, in Order to form a more perfect Union, establish Justice, insure domestic Tranquility, provide for the common defense, promote the general Welfare, and secure the Blessings of Liberty to ourselves and our Posterity, do ordain and establish this Constitution for the United States of America.

To understand complex writing, you have to take it apart. First find the main idea of the long sentence. It's the first and last part. Most of the main idea is easy to understand, except for *ordain*. If you look up the word in the dictionary, you know it means "to enact or put into effect."

We the People of the United States . . . do ordain and establish this Constitution for the United States of America.

The rest of the writing gives details about the main idea, or why the Constitution is being put into effect. You might need to look up *domestic* and *tranquility*.

- form a more perfect Union

- establish Justice

- insure domestic Tranquility

- provide for the common defense

- promote the general Welfare

- secure the Blessings of Liberty

···

Directions   Answer these questions on another sheet of paper. Use a dictionary if necessary.

1. What does "form a more perfect Union" mean?

2. What does "insure domestic Tranquility" mean?

3. What does "secure the Blessings of Liberty" mean?

4. Are these good reasons to start a nation? Which reason do you think is the most important?

Name _____ Date _____

Charts ···

A **chart** gives information in the form of a picture or list. Charts provide much information in a small space. They make it easy to compare information. A chart lists a group of facts. Charts help you learn facts quickly. Read this chart to learn about taxes in the United States.

Chart

Federal Taxes in the United States		
Year	Total Tax* (millions)	Total Tax per Person
1950	$ 39,443	$ 261
1960	92,492	516
1970	192,807	949
1980	517,112	2,278
1990	1,031,321	4,141
2000	2,025,218	7,196

*includes individual and corporate taxes, social insurance, excise taxes, estate and gift taxes, customs duties, and federal reserve deposits

In the chart, look at the label at the top of each **column** of figures. The first column says *Year*. The next column says *Total Tax (millions)*. Next to 1950 you find $39,443. This stands for $39,443 million, or $39,443,000,000. The zeros are left out to save space. If you read the chart across a **row**, you can find out the tax for one year. If you read down a column, you can see how taxes have gone up over the years.

Sometimes charts have footnotes, or more details about a certain topic. Find the * by *Total Tax*. Now find the * at the bottom of the chart. The part at the foot or bottom of the chart tells more about the total tax.

· ·

Directions | **Use the chart to answer the questions.**

1. How much in federal taxes was collected in 2000? (Remember, the number shown is in millions, so you need to add six zeros.)

_____

2. In which ten-year span did the tax per person rise the most?

_____

3. In which year was the tax per person the lowest?

_____

Name _____ Date _____

Time Lines ··

A **time line** is a kind of chart. Remember, a chart arranges facts in a way that makes them easy to read and understand. A time line shows the order of events along a vertical or horizontal line.

Look at the time line below. It shows one decade, the 1920s. A decade is 10 years. The year 1930 is not a part of the 1920s. Read the time line from left to right.

- Read the title of the time line carefully.
- Read the years in the time line. Then read all the labels in the time line.
- Use your finger to follow the movement of the time line.
- Be sure you know what information you need and what information the time line gives.

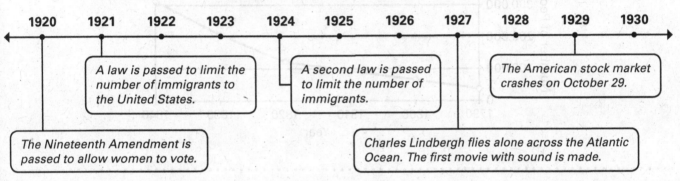

Important Events: 1920–1930

| 1920 | 1921 | 1922 | 1923 | 1924 | 1925 | 1926 | 1927 | 1928 | 1929 | 1930 |

A law is passed to limit the number of immigrants to the United States.

A second law is passed to limit the number of immigrants.

The American stock market crashes on October 29.

The Nineteenth Amendment is passed to allow women to vote.

Charles Lindbergh flies alone across the Atlantic Ocean. The first movie with sound is made.

· ·

Directions Use the time line to answer each question. Darken the circle by the correct answer.

1. How many years are in a decade?

  Ⓐ 1   Ⓒ 10

  Ⓑ 5   Ⓓ 100

2. In 1920, what was passed to give women the right to vote?

  Ⓐ the Nineteenth Amendment

  Ⓑ an immigration limit

  Ⓒ a sound movie

  Ⓓ the stock market

3. In which year did Charles Lindbergh fly alone across the Atlantic Ocean?

  Ⓐ 1924

  Ⓑ 1926

  Ⓒ 1927

  Ⓓ 1929

4. How many years passed between the passage of the Nineteenth Amendment and the stock market crash?

  Ⓐ 1   Ⓒ 7

  Ⓑ 3   Ⓓ 9

5. In which years were laws passed to limit the number of immigrants?

  Ⓐ 1921 and 1922

  Ⓑ 1921 and 1924

  Ⓒ 1923 and 1927

  Ⓓ 1927 and 1929

6. When was the Nineteenth Amendment passed compared to when the first movie with sound was made?

  Ⓐ before   Ⓒ the same year

  Ⓑ after   Ⓓ none of these

Graphs

A **graph** uses pictures, points, lines, bars, or areas to show and compare information. A **line graph** uses points and one or more lines to show information. A line graph can show how something changes over time. In most line graphs, a line going up means an increase; a line going down means a decrease. The line graph below shows how the population of New York City changed from 1790 to 1840.

To get the most from a line graph, first read the title of the graph. Then read the labels along the side and bottom. At the bottom left corner, the figures start at 0. They increase by 100,000 at each line. The dates go across the bottom of the graph. The dates show each ten years as the line moves to the right. The line shows how much the population of New York City increased over the years.

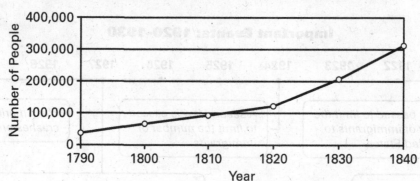

New York City's Population from 1790 to 1840

Directions Darken the circle by the best answer for each question.

1. What was New York City's population in 1820?
   Ⓐ 60,000
   Ⓑ 95,000
   Ⓒ 123,000
   Ⓓ 310,000

2. In which year was the population about 203,000 people?
   Ⓐ 1800
   Ⓑ 1810
   Ⓒ 1820
   Ⓓ 1830

3. What does the line graph suggest that many people began to do?
   Ⓐ move to the city
   Ⓑ move to farms
   Ⓒ leave the city
   Ⓓ die

4. What happened to the population of New York City between 1790 and 1840?
   Ⓐ stayed the same
   Ⓑ got smaller
   Ⓒ grew larger
   Ⓓ none of the above

CONTINUED ▶

Name _____ Date _____

Graphs, p. 2 ···

Another kind of graph is a **bar graph**. A bar graph shows how figures compare in size. The bar graph below compares the number of farm workers to the number of non-farm workers for every ten years between 1850 and 1900. The shading on the bars helps you see which bars represent which workers. It's easy to see that in 1880, for the first time, fewer people worked on farms than other places.

Farm Workers and Non-farm Workers, 1850–1900

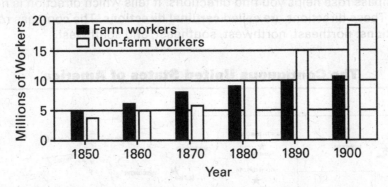

A **pie graph** or **circle graph** uses wedge-shaped "slices" to compare a part to the whole. The whole is always 100 percent. Each number becomes a slice of the whole pie. It's easy to compare the size of each piece or "slice" to the whole pie and to the other pieces. The pie graph on this page shows where people lived in the United States in 1900. It compares the number of people living in cities to the number of people living away from cities. The total population is 100 percent.

Population of United States in 1900

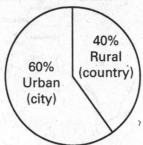

···

Directions Study the two graphs. Darken the circle by the answer that best completes each sentence.

1. In 1900, most people in the United States

   Ⓐ lived on farms.

   Ⓑ lived in cities.

   Ⓒ worked in factories.

   Ⓓ worked as farmers.

2. The number of farm workers and non-farm workers was about equal in

   Ⓐ 1870.

   Ⓑ 1880.

   Ⓒ 1890.

   Ⓓ 1900.

Maps ···

A **map** is a drawing of a place or area. Maps can tell about the boundaries of places, such as states or countries. They can tell about the landscape, the climate, the population, or many other things. All maps have a title to tell what the map shows.

Symbols on a map stand for real things. To learn what the symbols stand for, read the **map key**, or **legend**. A map may include a distance scale to tell how far apart places are. Most maps also have a **compass rose**. The compass rose helps you find directions. It tells which direction is north (N), east (E), south (S), or west (W). These directions are called **cardinal directions**. The compass rose may also show the **intermediate directions**: northeast, northwest, southeast, and southwest.

The Contiguous United States of America

···

Directions   **Use the map to answer the questions.**

1. What is the title of the map? _____

2. What does the star symbol in the legend mean? _____

3. In which state do you live? _____

4. What is the capital of your state? _____

5. Find Kentucky on the map. Which direction would you need to go from Kentucky to get to your state?

_____

CONTINUED ▶

Name _____ Date _____

Maps, p. 2 ···

Maps often use colors, shading, or patterns to tell details about a place. Some maps use pictures, too. You must pay close attention to read maps that use colors, shading, or patterns. You should find what each kind of shading means in the map key.

How to Read a Map with Shading or Patterns

1. Find the area you want to know about and note the shading or pattern in that area.

2. Match the shading or pattern on the map with the symbol in the map key.

Union States and Confederate States

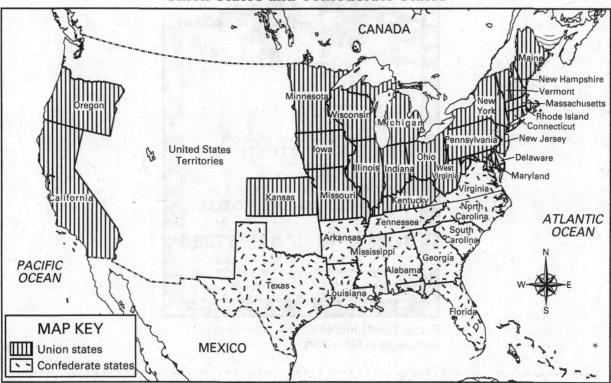

Directions | **Use the map to answer the questions.**

1. Was Missouri a Union state or a Confederate state? _____

2. Name a Union state on the West Coast. _____

3. Were there more Union states or Confederate states? _____

4. In which part of the country were most Confederate states located? _____

5. What is the large part of the United States that is not shaded? _____

Posters ···

A **poster** is a large graphic card or notice that is displayed in a public place. Posters can be used to advertise products. They can tell about artistic performances or candidates for election. Most posters include both words and pictures.

The words in biggest letters on the poster are usually the most important. On a campaign poster, the main candidate's name is in big letters. Whose name is in biggest letters on this poster?

A poster usually has pictures. A picture of a product, performer, or candidate might be on the poster. The pictures might be symbolic images, such as on this poster. What do the eagle and the shield symbolize?

Source: Library of Congress

Poster from Lincoln's 1864 presidential campaign in New York

···

| **Directions** | Use the poster to answer the questions. |

1. Who is running for president of the United States? _____

2. Who is running for vice president of the United States? _____

3. What office is Reuben Fenton seeking? _____

4. Would this poster make you vote for the candidates? Tell why or why not.

_____

_____

Photographs ···

A picture is worth a thousand words, the old saying goes. A **photograph** is an image captured on a sensitized surface, usually by a burst of light. Photographs can provide a record of history, both personal and public. Photographs can show us the history of the world. They can freeze actions in time. The photograph below is a famous picture taken by Joe Rosenthal during World War II in the Pacific.

To gain the most from a photograph, first pay attention to the images. What is in the center of the picture? What is in the foreground? What is in the background? Notice the use of light and dark in the photograph. What mood does the photographer establish?

A photograph may also have a **caption**. The caption gives written information about the photograph. What is the caption of this photograph?

Source: National Archives and Records Administration

Raising the Flag on Iwo Jima, February 23, 1945

··

Directions | Use the photograph and caption to answer the questions.

1. When was this photograph taken? _____

2. What is the central image of the photograph? _____

_____

3. How does the photograph make you feel? _____

_____

_____

_____

_____

Political Cartoons ·

A **political**, or editorial, **cartoon** is an illustration that contains a social or political message. The cartoon tries to make a point. Political cartoons usually require the reader to have some knowledge of current events.

Study the cartoon below. Political cartoonists often label things in the cartoon. Notice that the White House is labeled, and so is the suitcase. The suitcase, or bag of ideas, belongs to William Jennings Bryan. Bryan lost presidential elections in 1896, 1900, and 1908. The "16 to 1" on the bag refers to Bryan's economic ideas. He wanted to coin silver at a ratio of 16 to 1, giving the money little true value.

Source: National Archives and Records Administration

Mr. Bryan in 1899. "I stand where I stood three years ago!"

Directions | **Use the political cartoon to answer the questions.**

1. Is Bryan inside or outside the fence at the White House? _____

2. What does the cartoonist mean by placing Bryan there?

_____

_____

_____

_____

Using Documents ···

To get the most from a document, you should ask yourself questions about it.

- Where and when was the document written?

- Who created the document? Do you know anything about this person?

- What is the purpose of the document? Summarize the main idea.

- Who is the audience of the document? Do you know anything about this audience?

- Are there any unfamiliar words? Underline them. Look them up in a dictionary. The fun of learning is finding out.

- Does the document contain figurative language or symbols? What do they mean? Think about them awhile.

- Is the document effective? How does it influence the reader or viewer?

Try this famous quote:

> I only regret that I have but one life to lose for my country.
>
> —last words of Nathan Hale as he was being hanged, September 22, 1776

Read the credit line for important information.

Nathan Hale was an American spy during the Revolutionary War. He was caught by the British and hanged. He was only 21 years old.

··

Directions   Use the quote to answer the questions.

1. When was Nathan Hale hanged? _____

2. What can you tell about Nathan Hale from his quote?

_____

_____

3. If you were Nathan Hale, what would you say?

_____

_____

The Gettysburg Address ·····································

One of the great battles of the Civil War was fought at Gettysburg, Pennsylvania, in early July 1863. Over 50,000 Union and Confederate soldiers died in the battle. A military cemetery was built at Gettysburg for the thousands of Union soldiers who died there. The dedication of the cemetery took place on November 19, 1863. President Lincoln gave a short speech. Lincoln told Americans that the purpose of the Civil War was to make the United States a democracy with freedom and liberty for all. The Gettysburg Address lasted only two minutes, but today it is considered one of the nation's greatest speeches.

··

Directions Read the original speech and the explanation. Look up the unfamiliar words in dark print. Think about Lincoln's purpose for giving the speech.

Actual Gettysburg Address

Four score and seven years ago our fathers brought forth, upon this continent, a new nation, **conceived** in Liberty and dedicated to the **proposition** that all men are created equal.

Now we are engaged in a great civil war, testing whether that nation, or any nation so conceived and so **dedicated**, can long **endure**. We are met on a great battlefield of that war. We have come to dedicate a portion of that field, as a final resting place for those who here gave their lives that that nation might live. It is altogether fitting and proper that we should do this.

But, in a larger sense, we cannot dedicate—we cannot **consecrate**—we cannot **hallow**—this ground. The brave men, living and dead, who struggled here, have consecrated it, far above our poor power to add or **detract**. The world will little note, nor long remember what we say here, but it can never forget what they did here.

Explanation of the Gettysburg Address

Eighty-seven years ago, in 1776, our leaders created a new nation based on the idea of liberty. The United States would exist to prove the statement that "all men are created equal."

Now we are fighting a civil war. This war is a test to see if the United States, or any other nation, can exist for a long time if it is based on the ideas of liberty and equality. We are now meeting at the battlefield of Gettysburg. We have come to dedicate part of the battlefield as a cemetery for soldiers who died here. Those soldiers died fighting so that the United States would continue to be a nation based on ideas of liberty and equality. It is correct and proper that we dedicate this cemetery to honor those dead soldiers.

But we really do not have the power to dedicate this cemetery and make this ground holy. We cannot do this because this cemetery has already been made holy by the brave men, living and dead, who fought at Gettysburg. We cannot do anything more to make this cemetery holy than they have already done. The world will not notice or remember what we say here today. But the world can never forget what they did at Gettysburg.

CONTINUED ▶

The Gettysburg Address, p. 2 ·

Actual Gettysburg Address

It is rather for us the living, to be here dedicated to the unfinished work which they who fought here have thus far so nobly advanced. It is rather for us to be here dedicated to the great task remaining before us—that from these honored dead we take increased **devotion** to that cause for which they gave the last full measure of devotion—that we here highly **resolve** that these dead shall not have died in **vain**—that this nation, under God, shall have a new birth of freedom—and that government of the people, by the people, for the people, shall not perish from the earth.

Explanation of the Gettysburg Address

It must be our job to dedicate our own lives to the work these soldiers fought for so hard but could not finish. We must dedicate ourselves to the great cause for which these soldiers died. To honor them, we must work harder than ever for this cause. We must prove that these soldiers did not die without a reason. We must work hard so that this nation, under God, will have a government that allows equality and liberty for all people. We must make sure that this democratic government will never be destroyed.

· ·

Directions | Darken the circle by the best answer.

1. Why did people gather at Gettysburg on November 19, 1863?

- Ⓐ to fight
- Ⓑ to dig some graves
- Ⓒ to put up mailboxes
- Ⓓ to dedicate a cemetery

2. How long is four score and seven years?

- Ⓐ 11 years
- Ⓑ 1776 years
- Ⓒ 87 years
- Ⓓ 27 years

3. A proposition is _____.

- Ⓐ a part of an airplane
- Ⓑ a mistake
- Ⓒ an idea offered for acceptance
- Ⓓ a place to bury soldiers

4. In Lincoln's speech, *resolve* means to _____.

- Ⓐ make a firm decision
- Ⓑ solve again
- Ⓒ argue
- Ⓓ think about

· ·

Directions | Write complete sentences to answer the questions. Use a separate sheet of paper to write your answers.

5. Why do you think Lincoln gave this speech?

6. What do you think Lincoln meant when he said that the soldiers "gave the last full measure of devotion"?

7. What does Lincoln say the Union soldiers fought for?

8. How does Lincoln think Americans should finish the work for which the Union soldiers fought?

Kitty Hawk, North Carolina, 1903 ·····························

On December 17, 1903, Orville and Wilbur Wright made several powered flights. They are said to be the first men to fly. The longest flight of the day was the last one. Wilbur was the pilot that time, steering the clumsy biplane. Orville later wrote about the event in his diary.

Directions | Circle the time and distance references in the document. Can you see the event in your mind?

At just twelve o'clock Will started on the fourth and last trip. The machine started with its ups and downs as it had before, but by the time he had gone 300 or 400 feet he had it under much better control, and was travelling on a fairly even course. It proceeded in this manner till it reached a small hummock out about 800 feet from the starting ways, when it began pitching again and suddenly darted to the ground. The front rudder frame was badly broken up, but the main frame suffered none at all. The distance over the ground was 852 feet in 59 seconds.

Source: *Miracle at Kitty Hawk: The Letters of Wilbur and Orville Wright*, edited by Fred C. Kelly

Directions | Write complete sentences to answer the questions.

1. How far did the airplane travel on its last trip? How long did it stay in the air?

_____

2. Have you ever invented anything? What? How did you feel about your achievement?

_____

_____

3. How do you think the Wright brothers felt when their flying machine actually worked?

_____

_____

CONTINUED ▶

Name _____ Date _____

Kitty Hawk, North Carolina, 1903, p. 2 ·······················

How good are you at math? Can you figure out the average speed of the Wright plane on its last trip? It traveled 852 feet in 59 seconds. Hint: It's just under 10 miles per hour. Passenger jets fly over 500 miles per hour. But if you think the Wright plane was slow, just look at it. You can probably run as fast as it could fly.

The Wright Flyer, 1903

Over 100 years old, this picture of the Wright plane is dim and decaying. Like human flight, photography was in its early days in 1903.

· ·

Directions | **Use the Wright brothers' flight and the photograph to answer the questions.**

1. Why do you think the Wright brothers wanted to fly? _____

_____

2. What do you really want to do? Do you have a plan to accomplish your goal? _____

_____

_____

3. How are the Wright Flyer and a modern airplane alike? How are they different? _____

_____

_____

4. Is it important to preserve old things, such as this photograph of the Wright Flyer? Explain.

_____

_____

Name _____ Date _____

Before the Civil War ···

A chart lists a group of facts. You can compare facts by reading a chart. Look at the chart below. It compares the North and South before the Civil War. To learn facts about the North and the South, read the numbers listed under each heading. Read the chart from left to right to find out what the numbers in the chart stand for.

Read the title to see what information the chart contains.

Read the column headings to see what the information in the column refers to.

The North and South Before the Civil War		
	North	**South**
Money	$330,000,000	$47,000,000
Number of factories and shops	111,000	21,000
Miles of railroad track	22,000	9,000
Horses	3,400,000	1,700,000
Units of wheat	132,000,000	31,000

Read the row labels to see what the information in the row is about.

··

Directions   Darken the circle by the best answer for each question.

1. How many miles of railroad track did the South have before the Civil War?

   Ⓐ 22,000

   Ⓑ 9,000

   Ⓒ 21,000

   Ⓓ 31,000

2. How many factories and shops did the North have before the war?

   Ⓐ 3,400,000

   Ⓑ 22,000

   Ⓒ 111,000

   Ⓓ 21,000

3. How much money did the South have compared to the North before the war?

   Ⓐ more

   Ⓑ less

   Ⓒ the same amount

   Ⓓ none

4. How many units of wheat did the North have compared to the South before the Civil War?

   Ⓐ more

   Ⓑ fewer

   Ⓒ the same number

   Ⓓ none

··

Directions   Write complete sentences to answer the questions. Use another sheet of paper.

5. Based on the chart, how would you compare the North to the South before the Civil War? Was one stronger, or were they about equal in strength?

6. Which side would you expect to be more able to win a war? Explain.

Name _____ Date _____

Causes and Effects ··

A chart can also be used to give details about events. The chart on this page shows important events from 1990 to 2004. Each event caused certain effects, or results. Remember to read the title and headings carefully.

Read the date to see when each event occurred. ▶

Important Events from 1990 to 2004

Date	Event	Effects
1990	Congress passes the Americans with Disabilities Act.	Americans with disabilities have the same rights as other Americans.
1991	The cold war ends.	The United States is the strongest world leader.
1993	NAFTA is signed by the United States, Canada, and Mexico.	There are fewer tariffs among the three nations.
2001	Terrorists attack the World Trade Center and Pentagon.	The United States starts a war on terrorism.
2003	The United States goes to war against Iraq.	Saddam Hussein is no longer Iraq's dictator.
2003	Congress passes a law to help older Americans pay for medicine.	It is easier for older people to buy medicine.
2004	Americans vote for a new president.	George W. Bush wins the election.

◀ **Read the effect of each event.**

··

Directions   Use the chart to answer the questions. Write complete sentences.

1. In which year did the cold war end?

_____

2. What was the effect of the end of the cold war?

_____

3. What was the effect of the attack on the World Trade Center and Pentagon?

_____

_____

4. Which of these events do you think is the most important? Explain.

_____

_____

Name _____ Date _____

Time Line: 1860–1960 ······················

A time line shows the order of events in a certain period of time. The events and time they happen are presented along a vertical or horizontal line. This line shows the sequence of events. The time line below shows important events in Arizona history from 1860 to 1960.

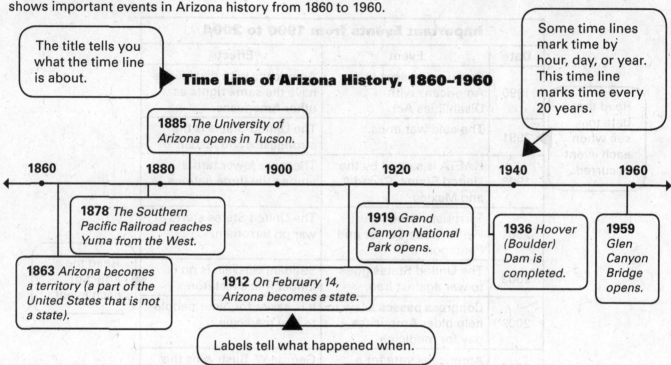

The title tells you what the time line is about.

Time Line of Arizona History, 1860–1960

Some time lines mark time by hour, day, or year. This time line marks time every 20 years.

1885 *The University of Arizona opens in Tucson.*

| 1860 | 1880 | 1900 | 1920 | 1940 | 1960 |

1878 *The Southern Pacific Railroad reaches Yuma from the West.*

1863 *Arizona becomes a territory (a part of the United States that is not a state).*

1912 *On February 14, Arizona becomes a state.*

1919 *Grand Canyon National Park opens.*

1936 *Hoover (Boulder) Dam is completed.*

1959 *Glen Canyon Bridge opens.*

Labels tell what happened when.

Directions Use the time line. Darken the circle by the answer that best completes each sentence.

1. The _____ reached Yuma in 1878.

  Ⓐ Grand Canyon

  Ⓑ Glen Canyon Bridge

  Ⓒ University of Tucson

  Ⓓ Southern Pacific Railroad

2. The University of Arizona opened in Tucson in

  Ⓐ 1863.

  Ⓑ 1885.

  Ⓒ 1919.

  Ⓓ 1959.

3. Before Arizona became a state,

  Ⓐ Grand Canyon National Park opened.

  Ⓑ Arizona became a territory.

  Ⓒ Hoover Dam was completed.

  Ⓓ Glen Canyon Bridge opened.

4. After Grand Canyon National Park opened,

  Ⓐ the University of Arizona opened.

  Ⓑ Arizona became a territory.

  Ⓒ Hoover Dam was completed.

  Ⓓ Arizona became a state.

Directions Write complete sentences to answer the question. Use another sheet of paper.

5. Are events easier to understand on a time line or in a paragraph of information? Explain.

Name _____ Date _____

Ups and Downs ···

A line graph shows how something changes over time. The line may go up and down to show increases or decreases. The line graph on this page shows how many workers belonged to unions from 1900 to 2000. As always, read the title and labels carefully so you know what information the graph contains.

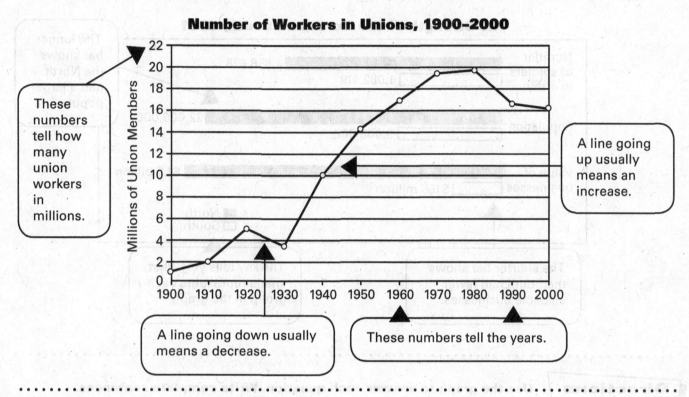

Number of Workers in Unions, 1900–2000

These numbers tell how many union workers in millions.

A line going up usually means an increase.

A line going down usually means a decrease.

These numbers tell the years.

···

| **Directions** | **Write complete sentences to answer the questions.** |

1. In 1910, about how many people belonged to unions?

_____

2. Between which years did union membership drop from about 5 million to less than 4 million?

_____

3. From 1930 to 1980, what happened to the number of people in unions?

_____

4. From 1980 to 2000, what happened to the number of people in unions?

_____

5. Based on the chart, do people in recent years seem interested in joining unions? Explain.

_____

_____

Name _____   Date _____

North and South in the Civil War ················

A bar graph shows how figures compare in size. A double bar graph gives information about two groups in each category. The double bar graph below compares the North and the South in strength at the beginning of the Civil War.

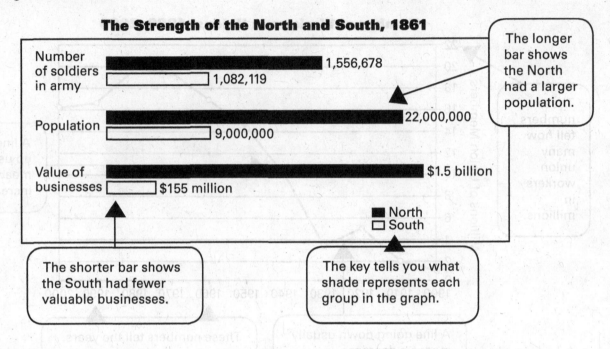

The Strength of the North and South, 1861

Number of soldiers in army: 1,556,678 / 1,082,119

Population: 22,000,000 / 9,000,000

Value of businesses: $1.5 billion / $155 million

■ North
□ South

The longer bar shows the North had a larger population.

The shorter bar shows the South had fewer valuable businesses.

The key tells you what shade represents each group in the graph.

···

Directions   Use the graph to answer each question. Write complete sentences.

1. How many more soldiers were in the Union Army (North) than in the Confederate Army (South)?

_____

2. Which side do you think was stronger at the beginning of the Civil War? Use the information from the bar graph to explain your answer.

_____

_____

_____

3. Compare this bar graph to the chart on page 24. Which makes the information easier to understand? Explain.

_____

_____

_____

_____

Name _____ Date _____

Comparing Graphs ·····································

Sometimes you will have to compare two graphs to determine how changes have occurred. As you remember, a pie graph uses slices to equal 100 percent. The two pie graphs below show where immigrants to the United States came from in 1900 and 1990. By comparing the two graphs, you can see changes in immigration patterns.

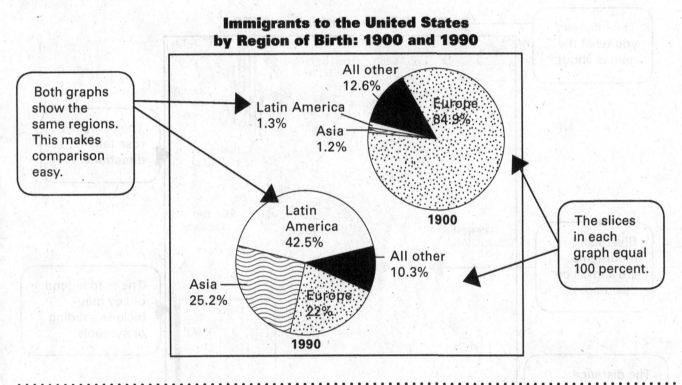

Immigrants to the United States by Region of Birth: 1900 and 1990

Both graphs show the same regions. This makes comparison easy.

The slices in each graph equal 100 percent.

···

Directions   Use the graphs to answer the questions. Write complete sentences.

1. Where did most immigrants to the United States come from in 1900?

_____

_____

2. Where did most immigrants to the United States come from in 1990?

_____

_____

3. Why do you think this change in immigration patterns might have occurred?

_____

_____

_____

4. Are pie graphs an easy way to compare information? Explain.

_____

_____

_____

Name _____ Date _____

Where Are We? ···

As you know, maps are a special kind of drawing of a place. Maps can show many types of information about a place. Maps can show borders, landforms, rivers, and routes. They can show population and precipitation. They can tell where events happened or where places are located. Learning to use maps well can help you find your way around the world. Maps can also help you learn more about history.

The title tells you what the map is about.

The compass rose tells directions.

Rivers and mountains are shown on this map.

The map legend or key may include shading or symbols.

The distance scale tells how far apart places are.

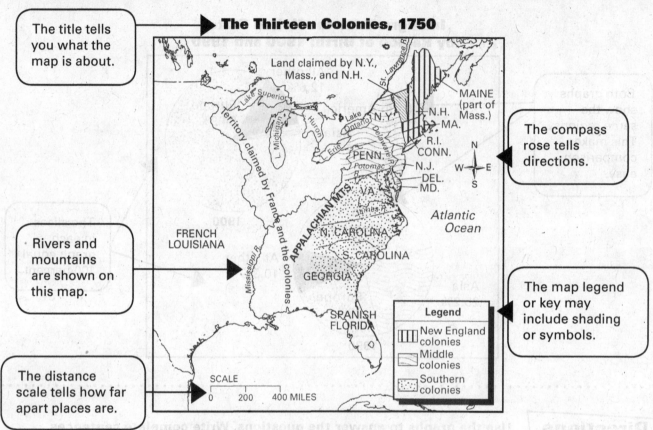

The Thirteen Colonies, 1750

···

Directions   **Use the map to answer the questions.**

1. Name a New England colony. _____

2. Which mountain range runs along the western border of North Carolina? _____

3. You want to travel from Pennsylvania to North Carolina. Which direction should you go?

_____

4. What country claimed the land west of the Mississippi River? _____

5. In what ways was the America of 1750 different from the United States of today?

_____

_____

_____

Name _____ Date _____

People and Places ·····································

Some maps give information about the people who live in places. Maps can tell how many people live in a place. They can tell how those people vote or work. They can also tell how they survive. The map on this page shows how Native American groups got their food about 400 years ago.

Food Sources of Native Americans Around 1600

<table>
</table>

··

Directions   Circle the compass rose, map key, and distance scale on the map. Then use the map to answer the questions.

1. What was the main food source of the Apache? _____

2. Name a group that depended on farming, hunting, and gathering. _____

3. How did most groups in the northern part of the continent get their food?

_____

4. What direction did the Cherokee live from the Shoshone? _____

5. Compare this map to the map of the thirteen colonies on page 30. How did the Native American groups in the area of the thirteen colonies get their food?

_____

6. How do you think the early colonists got their food? Explain.

_____

_____

_____

_____

Name _____   Date _____

Victims of War ···

Soldiers are not the only ones who suffer during war. Often the lives of civilians in war-torn areas are upset, too. Study the picture of these children in Naples, Italy, during World War II.

To get the most from a photograph, you must pay careful attention to the details of the image. Are there important details in the background? What is shown in the center of the photograph? What do you notice about the two boys in this photograph, especially the boy on the right? Is there a caption? What does it say?

Source: Corbis Royalty Free

Naples, Italy, during World War II

···

| **Directions** | Use the photograph to answer the questions. Write complete sentences. |

1. What do you notice about the two boys in the photograph?

_____

2. How does the photograph make you feel?

_____

_____

3. How do you think the photographer feels about war?

_____

_____

4. Do you think a photograph can make you feel or think a certain way? Explain.

_____

_____

Name _____ Date _____

The War Ends! Yippee!

On August 14, 1945, World War II ended. As the news spread, people were overjoyed that the long years of conflict were over. In Times Square in New York City, this couple celebrated with a famous kiss. This photograph was taken by Lt. Victor Jorgenson of the U.S. Navy.

Source: National Archives and Records Administration

Times Square, New York City, August 14, 1945

Directions | Use the photograph to answer the questions. Write complete sentences.

1. What is the central image in the photograph?

_____

_____

2. How do you think the other people in the photograph feel? How can you tell?

_____

_____

3. How does the photograph make you feel?

_____

_____

I Want You to Look at This Poster ·································

A poster tries to influence people. It can make people vote for a candidate or buy a certain product. Posters often have bright colors and bold images. The poster below was originally printed in red, white, and blue. It was created by James Montgomery Flagg to get people to help in the World War II effort.

Posters often contain symbols. Who is this man? What does he represent?

Posters often contain words. The words deliver the message of the poster.

World War II recruiting poster, 1941–1945

Directions Use the poster to answer the questions. Write complete sentences.

1. What does this poster try to get people to do?

_____

2. Who do you think is the target audience for the poster?

_____

_____

3. Who is the man in the picture? What does he represent?

_____

_____

4. Are the messages in the poster mostly visual or verbal or both? Describe the features that make the poster this way.

_____

_____

Name _____ Date _____

What's So Funny? ···

A political cartoon is an illustration that contains a social or political message. Often a political cartoon tries to make you think a certain way about an issue. Study the cartoon below. What is its message?

The sign tells you the cartoon is about an election.

This is a great town. This is a great year. All of you are wonderful people. So, in conclusion, I can only say, "Vote for me!"

What does he mean . . . in conclusion?

I didn't hear any facts leading up to that conclusion!

The listeners' thoughts suggest they do not trust the candidate.

···

Directions   Use the cartoon to answer the questions. Write complete sentences.

1. Why are the two listeners not satisfied with the speech?

_____

_____

2. Does the candidate give any good reasons voters should elect him?

_____

_____

3. What is the main idea of this political cartoon?

_____

_____

4. Is the cartoon effective in persuading the reader? Explain.

_____

_____

_____

_____

Enough Is Enough ·

Pancho Villa was a Mexican revolutionary and bandit. In 1916 and 1917, he and his men raided border towns in the United States. On March 9, 1916, they raided Columbus, New Mexico, and killed about 12 U.S. citizens. President Woodrow Wilson then ordered U.S. troops to pursue Villa into Mexico. See how the political cartoon below illustrates that event. The cartoon was drawn by Clifford Berryman.

Who is the man jumping the fence?

The fence is a symbol. What does it represent?

Notice the burning town and the torch in Villa's hand.

Source: National Archives and Records Administration

· ·

Directions Use the cartoon to answer the questions. Write complete sentences.

1. What does the fence in the cartoon represent?

_____

2. Who is the man jumping the fence? What does he represent?

_____

_____

3. Is the cartoon effective in making the reader believe that Villa should be chased? Explain.

_____

_____

_____

_____

Declare Your Independence ······················

In this unit, you will study documents on your own. Read or view each document carefully and then answer the questions.

> **Remember, to understand a text document:**
> • Find out when and where the document was created.
> • Find out about the person who created the document.
> • Find the purpose and main idea of the document.
> • Look up any unfamiliar words.

Following is the second paragraph of the Declaration of Independence. The Declaration was mainly written by Thomas Jefferson in the early summer of 1776. This paragraph contains some important ideas of our nation.

> We hold these truths to be self-evident: that all men are created equal, that they are endowed by their Creator with certain unalienable rights, that among these are life, liberty, and the pursuit of happiness.

· ·

Directions | First circle any unfamiliar words and look them up. Then write complete sentences to answer the questions.

1. What are "unalienable rights"?

_____

_____

2. What are the three unalienable rights mentioned in the Declaration of Independence?

_____

_____

3. Why are these three rights important for our nation?

_____

_____

_____

_____

_____

Which Would You Choose? ·····························

In 1775, the relationship between the American colonies and England was strained. Going to war against England was a common topic. On March 23, 1775, Patrick Henry delivered a famous speech to the leaders of the Virginia colony. A small part of that speech follows.

Patrick Henry

Gentlemen may cry, "Peace! Peace!"—but there is no peace. The war is actually begun! The next gale that sweeps from the north will bring to our ears the clash of resounding arms! Our brethren are already in the field! Why stand we here idle? What is it that gentlemen wish? What would they have? Is life so dear, or peace so sweet, as to be purchased at the price of chains and slavery? Forbid it, Almighty God! I know not what course others may take; but as for me, give me liberty, or give me death!

···

Directions   **Answer the questions on another sheet of paper. Write complete sentences.**

1. What are some unfamiliar words in the passage? Did you look them up in the dictionary?

2. What does Henry mean when he says, "The next gale that sweeps from the north will bring to our ears the clash of resounding arms!"?

3. What is Patrick Henry's main idea in the speech? Underline it.

4. Patrick Henry proclaims, "Give me liberty, or give me death!" Which would you choose if necessary?

5. Look at the picture of Patrick Henry. Does seeing the man change your feeling about his words? Can a speaker influence a listener as much as words can?

Name _____   Date _____

The Lincoln Assassination, 1865 ·························

Abraham Lincoln was assassinated by John Wilkes Booth on April 14, 1865. President Lincoln was attending a play with his wife. His physician wrote this report about a month later.

> I was sent for by Mrs. Lincoln immediately after the assassination. I arrived there in a very few moments and found that the President had been removed from the theatre to the house of a gentleman directly opposite the theatre, had been carried into the back room of the residence, and was there placed upon a bed. . . . I proceeded then to examine him, and instantly found that the President had received a gunshot wound in the back part of the left side of his head, into which I carried immediately my finger. I at once informed those around that the case was a hopeless one; that the President would die; that there was no positive limit to the duration of his life. . . .

Source: Testimony of Dr. Robert King Stone, May 16, 1865
National Archives and Records Administration

· ·

Directions Use the doctor's report to answer the questions. Write complete sentences.

1. When did Dr. Stone present his testimony?

_____

2. How does the report make you feel?

_____

3. What words or descriptions in the report make you feel this way?

_____

_____

4. The doctor was present when President Lincoln died. Does knowing this make you react more emotionally to the report? Explain.

_____

_____

_____

_____

_____

_____

Wounded Knee, 1890 ·······································

On December 29, 1890, U.S. Army soldiers killed about 300 Lakota Sioux at Wounded Knee, South Dakota. The Sioux had few weapons to fight back against the soldiers armed with Hotchkiss machine guns. The event marked the last major battle between the Native Americans and white people. Black Elk happened upon the scene later.

> I told the others to stay back, and I charged upon them holding the sacred bow out toward them with my right hand. They all shot at me, and I could hear bullets all around me, but I ran my horse right close to them, and then swung around. . . . I got back to the others and was not hurt at all. . . . We all charged on the soldiers. They ran eastward toward where the trouble began. We followed down along the dry gulch, and what we saw was terrible. Dead and wounded women and children and little babies were scattered all along there where they had been trying to run away. The soldiers had followed along the gulch, as they ran, and murdered them in there. Sometimes they were in heaps because they had huddled together, and some were scattered all along. Sometimes bunches of them had been killed and torn to pieces where the wagon-guns hit them. I saw a little baby trying to suck its mother, but she was bloody and dead.
>
> . . . When we drove the soldiers back, they dug themselves in, and we were not enough people to drive them out from there. In the evening they marched off up Wounded Knee Creek, and then we saw all that they had done there.

Source: *Black Elk Speaks*, as told to John Neihardt, 1932

···

| **Directions** | Use Black Elk's account of the events to answer the questions. Write complete sentences. |

1. How do you think Black Elk felt when he saw the scene?

_____

_____

2. What words or descriptions does he use to express his feelings?

_____

_____

_____

_____

_____

_____

A Different View of the Event ···············

A few days after the event at Wounded Knee, the following editorial appeared in the *Aberdeen Saturday Pioneer* in Aberdeen, South Dakota. It was written by a young editor named L. Frank Baum. About ten years later, Baum became famous for a book he wrote called *The Wonderful Wizard of Oz*.

Words, ideas, and beliefs change over time. Baum uses language and ideas in his editorial that would not be accepted today. However, Baum's view in this editorial was a common one in his time.

> The peculiar policy of the government in employing so weak and vacillating a person as General Miles to look after the uneasy Indians, has resulted in a terrible loss of blood to our soldiers, and a battle which, at its best, is a disgrace to the war department. There has been plenty of time for prompt and decisive measures, the employment of which would have prevented this disaster.
>
> The *Pioneer* has before declared that our only safety depends upon the total extermination of the Indians. Having wronged them for centuries we had better, in order to protect our civilization, follow it up by one more wrong and wipe these untamed and untamable creatures from the face of the earth. In this lies future safety for our settlers and the soldiers who are under incompetent commands. Otherwise, we may expect future years to be as full of trouble with the redskins as those have been in the past.

> An eastern contemporary, with a grain of wisdom in its wit, says that "when the whites win a fight, it is a victory, and when the Indians win it, it is a massacre."

Source: *Aberdeen Saturday Pioneer*, January 3, 1891

· ·

Directions   Use Baum's editorial to answer the questions. Write complete sentences. Use another sheet of paper.

1. What is Baum's opinion about the military leaders?

2. What is Baum's solution to the Indian problem?

3. Do you think Baum disliked American Indians? What words or ideas from the editorial suggest this? Explain.

4. Baum says that the Indians have been wronged for centuries. But he believes another wrong is a reasonable solution. Is his solution reasonable? Explain.

5. Do you think Baum really means what he says, or is he being ironic? Use evidence from the editorial to support your answer. Keep in mind that Baum's editorial was first published in 1891, not today.

My Fellow Americans ·········· ··

On January 20, 1961, John F. Kennedy became the new president of the United States. At the time, the United States was locked in a tense cold war with the Soviet Union. The threat of nuclear destruction was a common topic. In his inaugural speech, Kennedy called on Americans to come to the aid of their country.

Source: Photo No. W4/Spiegel in the John F. Kennedy Library

John F. Kennedy

. . . In the long history of the world, only a few generations have been granted the role of defending freedom in its hour of maximum danger. I do not shrink from this responsibility—I welcome it. I do not believe that any of us would exchange places with any other people or any other generation. The energy, the faith, the devotion which we bring to this endeavor will light our country and all who serve it—and the glow from that fire can truly light the world.

And so, my fellow Americans: ask not what your country can do for you—ask what you can do for your country. . . .

Source: John F. Kennedy's inaugural address, January 20, 1961

· ·

Directions | **Use Kennedy's speech to answer the questions. Write complete sentences.**

1. Does this portion of Kennedy's speech sound optimistic or fearful? What words or ideas suggest this feeling? Explain.

_____

_____

2. Think about what Kennedy meant by his last statement. Restate the last sentence in the speech in your own words.

_____

The Age of Invention ······································

The late 1800s and early 1900s were known as the Age of Invention. Many new devices were invented during this time. The chart below shows some of these inventions. Remember, charts provide much information in a small space. They make it easy to compare information. Charts help you learn facts quickly.

> **Remember, to get the most from a chart:**
> • Read the title to learn what the chart is about.
> • Read the column headings to learn what information is included.
> • Read all the information in the rows.

Inventions Change America

Inventor	Invention	Date	How the Invention Changed America
Alexander Graham Bell	telephone	1876	People who are far apart can talk to one another.
Thomas Edison	electric lightbulb	1879	Electric lights are used to light homes, streets, schools, and offices.
Jan Matzeliger	shoe-making machine	1882	Shoes are made in shoe factories and sold in shoe stores.
Orville and Wilbur Wright	airplane	1903	People can travel by airplane.
Henry Ford	assembly line to make cars quickly	1913	People travel in cars instead of on horses.

Directions Darken the circle by the answer that best completes each sentence.

1. To learn how the inventions changed America, read the chart from

Ⓐ left to right.

Ⓑ top to bottom.

Ⓒ right to left.

Ⓓ the middle.

2. To learn information about Thomas Edison, read the chart from

Ⓐ left to right.

Ⓑ right to left.

Ⓒ top to bottom.

Ⓓ bottom to top.

3. Using an assembly line to build cars was the idea of

Ⓐ Orville and Wilbur Wright.

Ⓑ Henry Ford.

Ⓒ Jan Matzeliger.

Ⓓ Alexander Graham Bell.

4. The Wright brothers invented the

Ⓐ telephone.

Ⓑ assembly line.

Ⓒ airplane.

Ⓓ shoe-making machine.

A World of Change ···································

The first half of the twentieth century was a time of upheaval and change. War and poverty were major factors that shaped the history of the United States during that time. Study the chart below to learn details about some of these events.

Important Events from 1914 to 1945

Event	Dates	What Happened?
World War I	1914–1918	The Allies and Central Powers fought. The Allies won.
Nineteenth Amendment passed	1920	Women in every state were allowed to vote.
Great Depression	1929–1939	The stock market crashed. Millions of people lost their jobs. Roosevelt and the New Deal created jobs for Americans.
World War II	1939–1945	The United States and the Allies fought against Germany, Italy, and Japan. The Allies won.

Directions | **Use the chart to answer the questions. Write complete sentences. Use another sheet of paper if necessary.**

1. In which year were women in every state finally allowed to vote?

_____

2. What were some of the effects of the Great Depression?

_____

_____

3. Which of these events do you think had the greatest effect on making the United States what it is today? Explain.

_____

_____

4. What is the most important event in U.S. history that has occurred in your lifetime? Tell what happened and why it is so important.

_____

_____

_____

_____

Time Line: 1925–1945 ·················· **45**

A time line shows the order of events in a certain period of time. The events and time they happened are presented along a vertical or horizontal line. This line shows the sequence of events. The time line below shows important events from 1925 to 1945.

> **Remember, to get the most from a time line:**
> - Read the title of the time line carefully.
> - Read all the labels in the time line.
> - Read the times or years in the time line.
> - Use your finger to follow the movement of the time line.

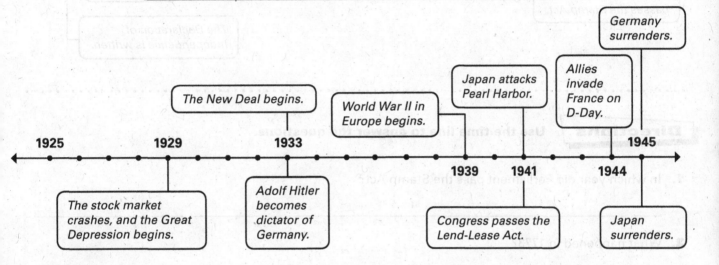

···

Directions | Use the time line to answer the questions. Darken the circle by the answer that best completes each sentence.

1. The stock market crash in _____ was the start of the Great Depression.

  Ⓐ 1925   Ⓒ 1933

  Ⓑ 1929   Ⓓ 1944

2. In 1933, _____ became the dictator of Germany.

  Ⓐ New Deal   Ⓒ Lend Lease

  Ⓑ Pearl Harbor   Ⓓ Adolf Hitler

3. The United States entered World War II after Japan attacked _____ on December 7, 1941.

  Ⓐ Europe   Ⓒ the stock market

  Ⓑ Pearl Harbor   Ⓓ Adolf Hitler

4. Thousands of Allied soldiers invaded France on _____ on June 6, 1944.

  Ⓐ New Deal Day   Ⓒ B-Day

  Ⓑ War Day   Ⓓ D-Day

···

Directions | Answer the question on another sheet of paper. Write complete sentences.

5. This time line shows many of the same events as the chart on page 44. Which graphic organizer makes the information easier to understand? Explain.

The Path to Revolution ···················

American colonists were upset with England long before the Declaration of Independence was written. Study the time line to learn some reasons why.

Events That Led to the Declaration of Independence

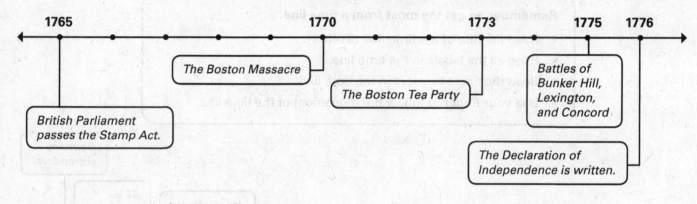

....

Directions   Use the time line to answer the questions.

1. In which year did Parliament pass the Stamp Act?

_____

_____

2. What happened in 1773?

_____

_____

3. In which year did three battles occur?

_____

_____

4. Do you think the American colonists were right to declare their independence? Explain.

_____

_____

_____

_____

_____

_____

_____

_____

46

Name _____ Date _____

The Vietnam War, 1965–1972 ·······························

The Vietnam War was a long, hard struggle. Many soldiers died there, and many Americans felt the United States should not be involved in the war. The bar graph shows the number of U.S. soldiers in Vietnam during the height of the Vietnam War.

Remember, to get the most from a graph:

• Read the title to see what the graph is about.

• Read the labels on the left and bottom of the graph to see what information is being presented.

• Be sure you understand what the lines, bars, or slices on a graph represent.

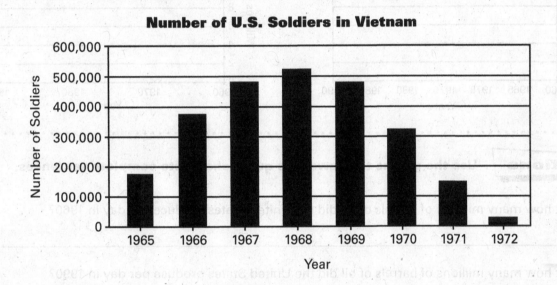

Number of U.S. Soldiers in Vietnam

Directions | Use the bar graph to answer the questions. Write complete sentences.

1. In which year were the greatest number of U.S. soldiers in Vietnam?

_____

2. What do you notice about the number of U.S. soldiers in Vietnam during the years 1965–1968?

_____

3. What do you notice about the number of U.S. soldiers in Vietnam during the years 1968–1972?

_____

4. Many Americans did not think the United States should be fighting the Vietnam War. Over 58,000 U.S. soldiers were killed there, and over 3 million Vietnamese people died during the struggle. Why do you think many Americans protested against the war?

_____

Name _____ Date _____

Fill It Up! ••

Sometimes you can use two graphs to compare two parts of the same topic. The line graphs below show how much oil was produced and how much was used in the United States per day from 1960 to 1990. Study the graphs to see how oil production and consumption have changed over time.

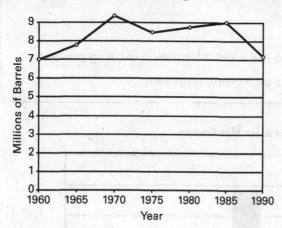

U.S. Oil Production, 1960–1990

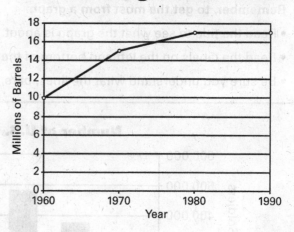

U.S. Oil Usage, 1960–1990

••

Directions Use the graphs to answer the questions. Write complete sentences.

1. About how many millions of barrels of oil did the United States produce per day in 1960?

_____

2. About how many millions of barrels of oil did the United States produce per day in 1990?

_____

3. How did U.S. oil production change between 1960 and 1990?

_____

4. About how many millions of barrels of oil did the United States use per day in 1960?

_____

5. About how many millions of barrels of oil did the United States use per day in 1990?

_____

6. What was the trend in U.S. oil usage between 1980 and 1990?

_____

7. During the years shown on the chart, did the United States ever produce as much oil as it consumed? What conclusion can you draw?

_____

_____

Women Win the Vote ·

Maps can tell many kinds of information. They can tell when events occurred in certain places. The map below shows when women gained the vote in the United States.

Remember, to get the most from a map:

- Read the title of the map to see what information the map presents.
- Find the compass rose. It tells directions on the map.
- Find the map legend or key. It tells what shading or symbols on the map mean.
- Find the distance scale. It tells how far apart places are.

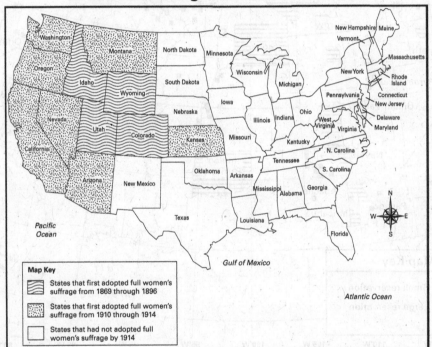

Women's Suffrage in the United States

Map Key

- States that first adopted full women's suffrage from 1869 through 1896
- States that first adopted full women's suffrage from 1910 through 1914
- States that had not adopted full women's suffrage by 1914

· ·

Directions   **Use the map to answer the questions.**

1. Name one of the four states in which women were first given the right to vote. _____

2. In which half of the country did women gain the right to vote last? _____

3. One half of the country gave women the right to vote before the other half did. What reasons can you think of to explain this?

_____

_____

Mapping the Past ··

The map below shows the locations of Native American reservations in 1875. The map also shows latitude and longitude lines. Lines of latitude run east and west. The equator is a line of latitude at 0°. All other lines of latitude are north or south of the equator. Lines of longitude run north and south. The prime meridian is a line of longitude at 0°. All the other lines of longitude are east or west of the prime meridian. The lines of latitude and longitude cross to form a grid. You can use the grid to locate places easily. For example, the Pyramid Lake Reservation is located at 40°N and 120°W. The two numbers are called coordinates. The line of latitude is always written first. Find these coordinates on the map. Circle the Pyramid Lake Reservation.

Native American Reservations, 1875

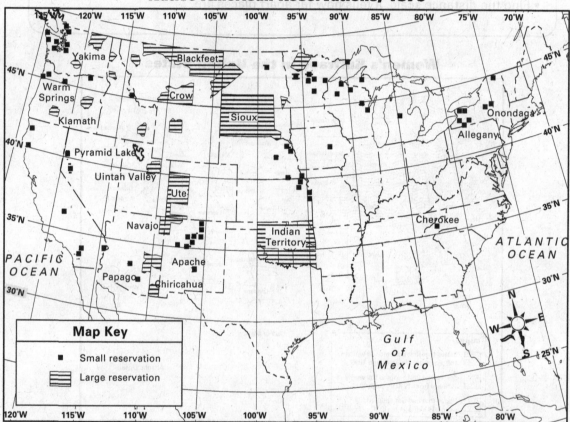

Directions | **Use the map to answer the questions.**

1. Are most of the large reservations in the eastern, western, or central part of the United States?

_____

2. What large reservation is located around 45°N and 100°W? _____

3. What are the coordinates of the Uintah Valley Reservation? Remember, lines of latitude are always

written first. _____

The Dust Bowl, 1930s ······························

During the 1930s, part of the Great Plains became a region called the Dust Bowl. When farmers planted wheat, they destroyed the prairie grass that held the soil on the Great Plains. Then came seven years of drought in the 1930s. The crops died, and the soil became dry and loose. Wind storms hit the Great Plains and blew dust off the dry fields. Thick dust buried farms, animals, cars, and houses. Dust storms also damaged other areas of the Great Plains.

One effect of the Dust Bowl disaster was a renewed effort to conserve the soil in the region. To prevent another dust bowl, thousands of trees have been planted to hold down the soil and block the wind on the Great Plains.

Sometimes maps are used to illustrate text. Notice how the map on this page gives more information about the topic.

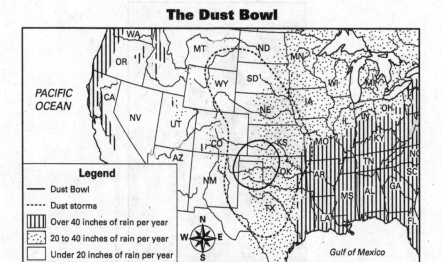

The Dust Bowl

Darken the circle by the best answer for each question.

1. Which of these states was not a part of the Dust Bowl?

Ⓐ Texas   Ⓒ Iowa

Ⓑ Oklahoma   Ⓓ Kansas

2. After the crops died,

Ⓐ the farmers planted wheat.

Ⓑ the prairie grass was destroyed.

Ⓒ seven years of drought came.

Ⓓ the soil became dry and loose.

Directions Read the text and study the map of the Dust Bowl. Then write complete sentences to answer the questions. Use another sheet of paper.

3. What caused the Dust Bowl? Write a brief summary.

4. What have people in this region done to prevent future dust bowls?

5. How does the map make the information easier to understand?

Name _____ Date _____

Keep Me Posted ·

Posters try to influence people. They try to make people do or not do something. Often posters will contain bold type and images. Look at the poster on this page. It was used as a recruitment poster during World War I. It tried to make men sign up for the navy. The poster was created by Howard Chandler Christy.

> **Remember, to get the most from a poster:**
>
> • Study the poster. To which words or images are your eyes drawn?
>
> • How is the main idea portrayed in the poster? What influences the viewer?
>
> • Think about the audience. Who would be influenced by this poster?

World War I recruiting poster, 1917–1918

· ·

Directions   **Use the poster to answer the questions. Write complete sentences.**

1. Who is the target audience of this poster?

_____

2. What words on the poster are emphasized? What effect do they have?

_____

3. What is the main idea of this poster?

_____

4. A young woman is portrayed on the poster. How might she influence the target audience?

_____

Voices: American History, SV 9781419036385

Name _____ Date _____

Dreadful Casuality! Outrage! ··

Today, people can communicate by TV, radio, telephone, and Internet. People in 1839 had none of those things. In 1839, most communication was done by newspapers, by word of mouth, or by posters. Look at the poster below. It tried to rally people against a railroad being built in Philadelphia in 1839.

Source: National Archives and Records Administration

··

Directions   **Write complete sentences to answer the questions. Use another sheet of paper.**

1. Notice the words in the darkest type. How do those words try to influence the reader?

2. Is the persuasive appeal of the poster emotional or logical? Use evidence from the poster to support your answer.

3. Would this poster influence you? Why or why not?

4. How would your life be different if you lived in 1839?

The March on Washington, 1963 ·······································

On August 28, 1963, over 250,000 people took part in a protest in Washington, D.C. The protest was called the March on Washington for Jobs and Freedom. The people came to Washington demanding better social conditions. The photograph on this page was taken near the Washington Monument.

Washington, D.C., August 28, 1963

···

Directions | **Use the photograph to answer the questions. Write complete sentences.**

1. Where and when was this photograph taken?

_____

2. What does this photograph tell you about the size of the crowd at the March on Washington?

_____

3. Why do you think all these people took part in the March on Washington for Jobs and Freedom?

_____

_____

_____

_____

In the Shadow of Lincoln ··

The March on Washington for Jobs and Freedom drew over a quarter of a million people to the nation's capital on August 28, 1963. In the photograph on this page, the leaders of the march pose before the statue of Abraham Lincoln in the Lincoln Memorial. In the first row, second from the right, is Martin Luther King, Jr.

Washington, D.C., August 28, 1963

Source: National Archives and Records Administration

· ·

Directions   **Use the photograph to answer the questions. Write complete sentences.**

1. What does this photograph tell you about the leaders of the March on Washington?

_____

2. Why is this photograph of the leaders at the feet of Lincoln symbolic or significant?

_____

_____

_____

_____

_____

_____

Convincing Cartoons ···

A political cartoon is an illustration that contains a social or political message. A political cartoon tries to make you think a certain way about a current issue. Study the cartoon below. What is its message?

> **Remember, to get the most from a political cartoon:**
>
> • Study the images and words in the cartoon. Important labels are often included.
>
> • Symbols are often used in political cartoons. Try to figure out what the symbols mean.
>
> • Some cartoons have captions or voice bubbles. Do you believe what is being said?

"Of course campaign contributions have no effect on my legislation."

··

Directions | Use the political cartoon to answer the questions. Write complete sentences. Use another sheet of paper.

1. Who is pouring money into the politician's pocket? Why do you think this person is giving money to the politician?

2. Why are the people with signs behind a fence? Who do they represent? Do they have access to the politician as the lobbyist does?

3. One sign says, "No Pork Barrel Legislation." What is "pork barrel" legislation?

4. Do you believe the caption that campaign contributions do not affect legislation?

5. What is the main idea of this cartoon? Is the cartoon effective in presenting that idea?

Separation of Powers ···

The Federal Bureau of Investigation, or FBI, is part of the Department of Justice. The Department of Justice is part of the executive branch of the federal government. In the late 1940s, Congress wanted to use the FBI to investigate communist activities in the government. The cartoon suggests that President Truman would not allow such use. Later, the Congressional investigation of "un-American activities" became known as McCarthyism, after Senator Joseph McCarthy of Wisconsin. This cartoon was drawn by Clifford Berryman in 1948.

Hope This Won't Develop Into a Neighborhood Feud, May 18, 1948

Source: National Archives and Records Administration

··

Directions | Use the political cartoon to answer the questions. Write complete sentences. Use another sheet of paper.

1. When was this political cartoon first published?

2. Who do the two men in the cartoon represent?

3. What does the fence in the cartoon represent?

4. Why does President Truman tell Congress to stay on its side of the fence?

5. Why is the separation of powers in the federal government important?

The San Francisco Earthquake, 1906 ·····························

You may be asked to study several documents about a topic. Then you may need to answer questions or write an essay about the documents. The rest of this unit will give you practice in this process.

To do your best:

• Study each document carefully.

• Read all titles and labels, and study all images.

• Think about how the documents fit together and the information they present about the topic.

• Think about all the documents as you answer the questions or write the essay.

On April 17, 1906, San Francisco, California, was struck by a massive earthquake. Fires burned for days after the earthquake struck, and over 28,000 buildings were destroyed. Over 700 people died, and about 250,000 people lost their homes. The photograph below shows destroyed buildings in the city.

Source: National Archives and Records Administration

Destroyed buildings in San Francisco, April 1906

···

Directions | **Write complete sentences to answer the question.**

1. What does the photograph show about the destruction of San Francisco?

_____

_____

_____

_____

CONTINUED ▶

The San Francisco Earthquake, 1906, p. 2 ·······················

Jack London, the famous writer, was in San Francisco during the earthquake. He later wrote about the destruction.

San Francisco is gone! Nothing remains of it but memories and a fringe of dwelling houses on the outskirts. . . . The factories and warehouses, the great stores and newspaper buildings, the hotels and the palaces . . . are all gone. . . .

Within an hour after the earthquake shock, the smoke of San Francisco's burning was a lurid tower visible a hundred miles away. And for three days and nights this lurid tower swayed in the sky, reddening the sun, darkening the sky, and filling the land with smoke.

On Wednesday morning at a quarter past five came the earthquake. A minute later the flames were leaping upward. In a dozen different quarters south of Market Street, in the working-class ghetto, and in the factories, fires started. There was no opposing the flames. There was no organization, no communication. All the cunning adjustments of a twentieth-century city had been smashed by the earthquake. The streets were humped into ridges and depressions and piled with debris of fallen walls. The steel rails were twisted into perpendicular and horizontal angles. The telephone and telegraph systems were disrupted. And the great water mains had burst. All the shrewd contrivances and safeguards of man had been thrown out of gear by thirty seconds' twitching of the earth-crust.

Source: Jack London's "The San Francisco Earthquake," *Collier's Weekly*, May 5, 1906

·····························

Directions
Answer the questions. Use another sheet of paper if necessary.

1. Good description creates vivid images in the reader's mind. Underline some of the vivid images in Jack London's report.

2. How do the photograph and the eyewitness account by London make the earthquake more real for the reader? Use evidence from the two documents to explain.

_____

_____

_____

3. The people who created these documents were present as history happened. What historical event would you choose to attend? Tell why.

_____

_____

_____

Name _____ Date _____

The Revolutionary War Begins ·······························

By 1775, the American colonists were long weary of England's political rule. Skirmishes broke out across the countryside as Patriots and Minutemen rushed to defend their rights and their country. Study these documents to learn more about this exciting time in U.S. history. Use the documents to answer the questions.

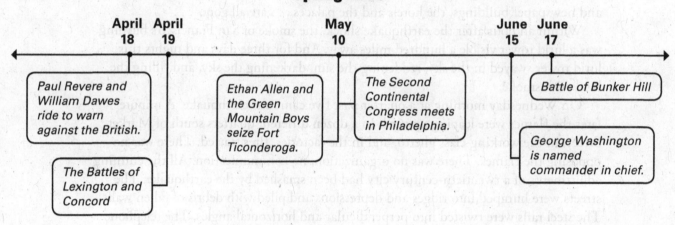

Spring 1775

| April 18 | April 19 | May 10 | June 15 | June 17 |

Paul Revere and William Dawes ride to warn against the British.

The Battles of Lexington and Concord

Ethan Allen and the Green Mountain Boys seize Fort Ticonderoga.

The Second Continental Congress meets in Philadelphia.

Battle of Bunker Hill

George Washington is named commander in chief.

···

Directions Use the time line to answer the questions.

1. What famous event occurred on April 18? _____

2. When did the battles of Concord and Lexington take place? _____

3. What happened soon after George Washington was named commander in chief?

_____

4. Suppose you are called upon to defend your rights and country. What would you do? How would you react?

_____

_____

_____

_____

_____

_____

_____

CONTINUED ▶

Name _____ Date _____

The Revolutionary War Begins, p. 2 ·······························

Many of the early battles in the Revolutionary War took place near Boston. The map below shows the Boston area.

Battles near Boston, 1775–1776

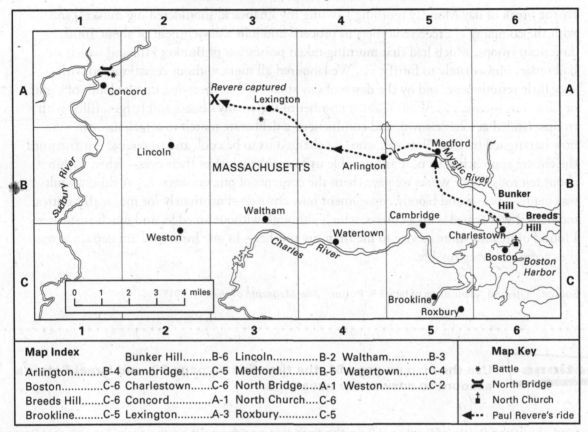

Map Index

	Bunker Hill........B-6	Lincoln.............B-2	Waltham............B-3
Arlington.........B-4	Cambridge.........C-5	Medford..........B-5	Watertown.........C-4
Boston............C-6	Charlestown......C-6	North Bridge.....A-1	Weston.............C-2
Breeds Hill......C-6	Concord............A-1	North Church....C-6	
Brookline.........C-5	Lexington..........A-3	Roxbury............C-5	

Map Key

*	Battle
✕	North Bridge
♱	North Church
◄- - -	Paul Revere's ride

··

Directions   Use the map on this page and the time line on page 60 to answer the questions.

1. Find the symbol for a battle in the map key. Some of the battles in the time line are on the map. Circle them.

2. Find the distance scale on the map. How far apart are Concord and Lexington? _____

3. Most of the Battle of Bunker Hill was fought on nearby Breeds Hill. Find the two places on the map.

   About how far apart are the two hills? _____

4. Find the symbol for Paul Revere's ride in the map key. About how far did Paul Revere ride? _____

5. Suppose you heard that a battle with the enemy was happening five miles away. What would you do?

   _____

   _____

CONTINUED ▶

The Revolutionary War Begins, p. 3 ····································

Israel R. Potter was one of the men who answered the call of his country. He fought in the Battle of Bunker Hill and later wrote this account:

> By the break of day Monday morning I swung my knapsack, shouldered my musket, and with the company . . . received orders to proceed and join a detachment of about 1000 American troops, which had that morning taken possession of Bunker Hill and which we had orders immediately to fortify. . . . We laboured all night without cessation and with very little refreshment, and by the dawn of day succeeded in throwing up a redoubt of eight or nine rods square. . . . About noon, a number of the enemy's boats and barges, filled with troops, landed at Charlestown, and commenced a deliberate march to attack us—we were now harangued by Gen. Putnam, who . . . charged us to be cool, and to reserve our fire until the enemy approached so near as to enable us to see the white of their eyes—when within about ten rods of our works we gave them the contents of our muskets. . . . A third assault was made—a close and bloody engagement now ensued—Fortunately for me, at this critical moment, I was armed with a cutlass, which although without an edge, and much rust-eaten, I found of infinite more service to me than my musket—in one instance I am certain it was the means of saving my life.

Source: "Life and Adventures of Israel R. Potter," *The Magazine of History*, 1911

· ·

Directions | **Use the map on page 61, the time line on page 60, and Israel Potter's account to answer the questions.**

1. You read about the Battle of Bunker Hill on the time line and found it on the map. Does Israel Potter's narrative make the battle seem more real to the reader? Explain.

_____

_____

_____

2. Which of these three documents is more effective in telling about history? Give reasons for your choice.

_____

_____

_____

_____

_____

Practice Test ·······································

You will probably have to take tests about historical documents. Learn how by using this practice test. Study each document carefully. You will be using all the documents to write an essay at the end of the test.

· ·

Directions | This practice test is based on documents 1 through 6. It will test your ability to work with historical documents. In Part A, look at each document and answer the question or questions after it. Use your answers to the questions in Part A to help you write your essay in Part B.

Historical Background

Soon after their arrival, Europeans started bringing enslaved Africans to North America. In 1700, there were 28,000 slaves in the British colonies. This shameful practice grew quickly. It was spurred on by the need for labor in an agricultural economy. By 1790, the population of the young United States included almost 700,000 enslaved people.

· ·

Directions | For **Part A**, study EACH document carefully and answer the question or questions after it. These answers will help you write your essay.

For **Part B**, use the information from the documents, your answers from Part A, and your knowledge of social studies to write a well-organized essay. The focus of your essay will be slavery and its opponents in the United States between 1790 and 1860.

Source: Library of Congress

Life in a slave cabin

GO ON ▶

Name _____ Date _____

Part A: Short-Answer Questions ·····················

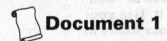 **Directions** The following documents show information about slavery in the United States between 1790 and 1860. Study each document carefully. Then answer the question or questions that follow it in the space provided.

In the 1700s, a trade route sprang up between British colonies in North America, Africa, and the West Indies. Because the trade route formed a three-sided figure, it was called the Triangular Trade.

Document 1

Triangular Trade

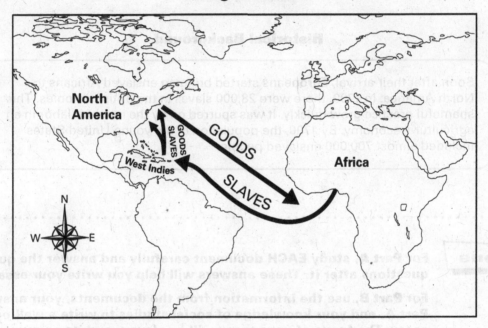

··

Directions Use the map to answer the questions. Write complete sentences.

1. What did ships from New England carry to Africa on the first leg of the journey?

_____

2. In Africa, what did the traders receive in exchange for their cargo?

_____

3. Where were slaves taken before they were brought to the British colonies in North America?

_____

GO ON ▶

Name _____ Date _____

From the West Indies, captured Africans were taken to the British colonies (later the United States). There they were sold into slavery. The enslaved population grew rapidly between 1790 and 1820.

Document 2

Enslaved Population of the 13 Original States

	1790	1820
New England States	3,763	145
Middle Atlantic States	45,210	22,365
Southern States	632,804	1,111,490
Total Enslaved Population	681,777	1,134,000

Source: U.S. Census Bureau

Directions Use the chart to answer the questions. Write complete sentences.

1. In what part of the country were almost all enslaved people found in both 1790 and 1820?

_____

2. In what two parts of the country did the enslaved population decrease between 1790 and 1820?

_____

3. In what part of the country did the enslaved population almost double between 1790 and 1820?

_____

GO ON ▶

Unit 3: Listening on Your Own
Voices: American History, SV 9781419036385

The Industrial Revolution reached the United States in the late 1700s. People in the South, however, did not build factories. They continued to use agriculture as their main way of life. Cotton was the most important crop. Many workers were needed to pick the cotton.

 Document 3

Source: Arkansas History Commission

. . . .

Directions Use the photograph and the text to answer the questions. Write complete sentences.

1. What kind of work are the enslaved people in the picture doing?

_____

_____

2. How do you know that this is very hard work? Use details from the picture to support your main idea.

_____

_____

_____

3. What do you think life was like for a slave?

_____

_____

_____

GO ON ▶

Enslaved people had no rights. One of the worst injustices of the system was the effect it had on families. Many tried to escape. Slaveholders advertised in newspapers for the return of runaways.

 Document 4

Source: *Jackson Telegraph,*
September 14, 1838

Source: *Richmond Enquirer,*
February 20, 1838

"Committed to the jail of Madison County, a negro woman, who calls her name Fanny, and says she belongs to William Miller, of Mobile. She formerly belonged to John Givins, of this county, who now owns several of her children."

"**Stop the Runaway!!!—$25 Reward.** Ran away from the Eagle Tavern, a negro fellow, named Nat. He is no doubt attempting to follow his wife, who was [just] sold to a [slave trader] named Redmond. The above reward will be paid by Mrs. Lucy M. Downman, of Sussex County, Virginia."

Directions Use the newspaper excerpts to answer the questions. Write complete sentences.

1. How much was the reward for the runaway slave named Nat?

_____

_____

2. How would you summarize the effect that slavery had on enslaved families? Give examples from the newspaper advertisements.

_____

_____

_____

_____

_____

_____

_____

_____

_____

_____

GO ON ▶

Name _____ Date _____

Industry became a chief economic activity in Northern states. Factories did not rely on slave labor. Over time, antislavery feelings became strong in these states. Abolitionists, people who wanted to end slavery, led the fight.

From 1790 on, the Abolitionist Movement gained strength in Northern states. Around 1820, abolitionist literature began to appear. From that time on, proslavery and antislavery groups continually struggled against each other. It would take another 45 years and a civil war, but the abolitionists would end slavery in America.

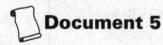 **Document 5**

Antislavery Actions

late 1700s	Leaders such as Thomas Jefferson and Patrick Henry speak out against slavery.
early 1800s	The American Colonization Society stages protests against slavery.
1831	William Lloyd Garrison publishes his newspaper, *The Liberator*. The newspaper speaks out against slavery and demands freedom for all slaves.
1833	The American Anti-Slavery Society is founded.

Directions | Use the text and the chart to answer the questions. Write complete sentences.

1. When was *The Liberator* first published?

_____

2. What was happening about slavery from the late 1700s through 1833? Use examples from the chart in your answer.

_____

_____

_____

_____

_____

_____

_____

_____

_____

_____

GO ON ▶

The Kansas-Nebraska Act of 1854 did not do much to solve the slavery problem in the United States. If anything, it made matters worse. The act repealed the Missouri Compromise of 1820. The Missouri Compromise had tried to maintain an equal balance between free states and slave states. The act also allowed the people of the new Kansas and Nebraska territories to vote whether to allow slavery. The act created many conflicts and eventually led the nation to civil war in 1860.

Document 6

Kansas-Nebraska Act of 1854

Map Key
- Free state or territory
- Slave state
- Area in which voters can vote on slavery issue

Directions   Use the map to answer the questions.

1. Where were most of the free states located? _____

2. Where were most of the slave states located? _____

3. Is your state shown on the map? If so, was it a free state or a slave state? _____

4. Find the Kansas and Nebraska territories on the map. They are very large. Why might slavery in those territories be unacceptable to those who opposed slavery?

_____

_____

_____

_____

_____

GO ON ▶

Part B: Essay ···

Directions | Write a well-developed essay about slavery in the United States between 1790 and 1860. Include an introduction, supporting paragraphs, and a conclusion. Use the documents on pages 64–69, your answers to the questions in Part A, and your knowledge of social studies to help you organize your ideas. Use your own paper to write the essay.

In your essay, remember to discuss:

- how and why Africans first came to the British colonies/United States
- the numbers of enslaved Africans in the United States in 1790 and 1820
- why so many slaves were found in one region
- what life was like for enslaved people and the effect on their families
- the rise of the antislavery movement in the 1800s

After you complete your essay, look at the following list and check your writing. Go back and make any corrections to your essay that might be needed.

- Did you remember to answer ALL parts of the question in your essay?
- Did you use as many documents as you could in your essay?
- Did you include information you already knew about the topic?
- Did you express yourself clearly?
- Did you stay on the topic and not add any unnecessary information?
- Did you write an introduction that explains what your essay is about?
- Did you write a conclusion that sums up what you wrote about in your essay?

After you have revised your essay, compare it to the sample essay on the next page.

Sample Top Score Essay ··

The following essay answers all of the parts of the writing task and uses the documents and some outside information. It develops ideas well, has good organization, and expresses ideas clearly. It would receive a top score. Compare this sample essay to your essay about slavery.

Slavery existed in this country for several hundred years. Europeans first brought slaves they captured in Africa to the British colonies. Ships from New England carried goods to Africa. They traded those goods for African people, and the ships took the Africans to the West Indies. From these islands, the Africans were sold into slavery in the colonies. This was called the Triangular Trade because the route formed a three-sided figure. This route is shown in Document 1.

> **Include specific evidence in your essay.**

In 1790, there were about 680,000 slaves in the United States. By 1820, there were more than one million. Document 2 shows how quickly the slave population grew. Almost all of the slaves were in the Southern states.

People in the South did not build factories. They relied on agriculture. Cotton was the most important crop. Most slaves picked cotton in the fields. It was very hard work. They had to carry heavy baskets and bend over in the fields all day under the sun. Even very young children had to help. Document 3 is an example of slaves working hard in the cotton fields.

> **Identify the documents you have used to write the essay.**

Enslaved people had no rights. Slavery had a terrible effect on slave families. Husbands and wives were sold to different owners. Mothers were sold to new owners, but their children could not go with them. Many slaves tried to escape, and owners offered rewards for their return. The advertisements in Document 4 show how poorly slaves were treated.

People in the Northern states built factories. They did not use much slave labor. Around 1790, people called abolitionists began a fight to end slavery. The abolitionists gained strength in the 1800s, as shown in Document 5. Leaders such as Thomas Jefferson and Patrick Henry, as well as the American Colonization Society, William Lloyd Garrison, and the American Anti-Slavery Society, all played a big part.

After 1820, proslavery and antislavery forces struggled for power. The Missouri Compromise of 1820 tried to keep free states and slave states in balance. But the Kansas-Nebraska Act of 1854 repealed that compromise. This act allowed the people of the new territories to vote on slavery. Even more conflicts followed. The map in Document 6 shows the free and slave states and the size of the new territories. The abolitionists finally won the struggle, but it took a long time and a civil war before slavery ended.

Practice Test 1 ··

Directions This practice test is based on documents 1 through 3. It will test your ability to work with historical documents. In Part A, look at each document and answer the question or questions after it. Use your answers to the questions in Part A to help you write your essay in Part B.

Historical Background

In 1803, the United States bought a large central part of the country from France. This area became known as the Louisiana Purchase. President Thomas Jefferson chose two men, Meriwether Lewis and William Clark, to lead an expedition to explore the new territory. The expedition, called the Corps of Discovery, started up the Missouri River on May 14, 1804. The expedition reached the Pacific Ocean on November 18, 1805. After a journey of 28 months, the explorers returned to St. Louis on September 23, 1806. The expedition provided detailed information about this new part of the United States.

··

Directions For **Part A**, study EACH document carefully and answer the question or questions after it. These answers will help you write your essay.

For **Part B**, use the information from the documents, your answers from Part A, and your knowledge of social studies to write a well-organized essay. The focus of your essay will be the Louisiana Purchase and the Lewis and Clark expedition in the early part of the 1800s.

Source: Library of Congress

Lewis and Clark at the Mouth of the Columbia River, 1805, by Frederic Remington

GO ON ▶

Name _____ Date _____

Part A: Short-Answer Questions ································

The following documents give information about the **Louisiana Purchase and the Lewis and Clark expedition** in the early part of the 1800s. Study each document carefully. Then answer the question or questions that follow it.

Document 1

> We set out early, ran on a log, and were detained one hour, proceeded the course of last night two miles to the mouth of a creek on the starboard side, called *Osage Woman's River*, about 30 yards wide, opposite a large island and a settlement. On this creek 30 or 40 families are settled.
>
> Stopped about one mile above for Captain Lewis, who had ascended the cliff which is at said cave, three hundred feet high, hanging over the waters. The water excessively swift today. We encamped below a small island in the middle of the river. Sent out two hunters. One killed a deer.
>
> This evening we examined the arms and ammunition. Found those men's arms in the pirogue in bad order. A fair evening. Captain Lewis near falling from the pinnacles of rocks, 300 feet. He caught at 20 feet.

Source: Captain William Clark, 23 May 1804, from *The Journals of Lewis and Clark*, Chapter 1, "Setting Forth"

··

Directions Use the journal excerpt to answer the questions. Write complete sentences.

1. Who wrote this part of the journal, and on what date?

_____

2. How does the journal excerpt suggest the members of the expedition got much of their food?

_____

_____

3. What are some of the dangers the men encountered on their expedition?

_____

_____

_____

GO ON ▶

Name _____ Date _____

The map below shows the Louisiana Purchase and the route of the Lewis and Clark expedition.

 Document 2

The Lewis and Clark Expedition, 1804–1806

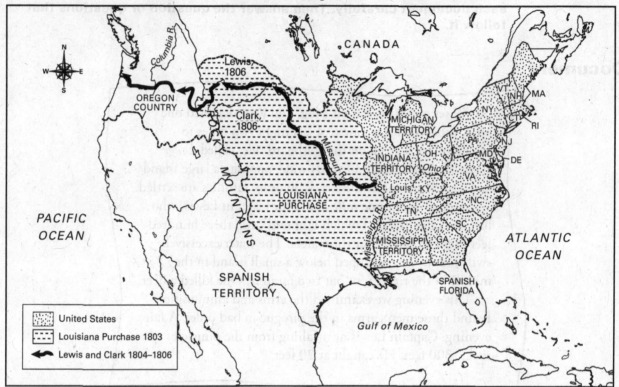

....

Directions   Use the map to answer the questions.

1. From which city did Lewis and Clark begin their trip?

_____

2. In which two general directions did the expedition head on its way to the Pacific Ocean?

_____

3. What effect did the Louisiana Purchase have on the size of the United States?

_____

4. Where did most of the people in the United States live before the Louisiana Purchase?

_____

GO ON ▶

Document 3

After refreshing ourselves, we proceeded on to the top of the dividing ridge, from which I discovered immense ranges of high mountains still to the west of us, with their tops partially covered with snow. I now descended the mountain about 3/4 of a mile, which I found much steeper than on the opposite side, to a handsome bold running creek of cold, clear water. Here I first tasted the water of the great *Columbia River*.

After a short halt of a few minutes, we continued our march along the Indian road which led us over steep hills and deep hollows to a spring on the side of a mountain where we found a sufficient quantity of dry willow brush for fuel. Here we encamped for the night. As we had killed nothing during the day, we now boiled and ate the remainder of our pork, having yet a little flour and parched meal.

This morning Captain Clark set out early. Found the river shoaly, rapid, shallow, and extremely difficult. The men in the water almost all day. They are getting weak, sore, and much fatigued. They complained of the fatigue to which the navigation subjected them and wished to go by land. Captain Clark encouraged them and pacified them. One of the canoes was very near oversetting in a rapid today. They proceeded but slowly.

Source: Captain Meriwether Lewis, 12 August 1805, from *The Journals of Lewis and Clark*, Chapter 16, "Here I First Tasted the Water of the Great Columbia River"

Directions Use the journal excerpt to answer the questions. Write complete sentences.

1. Who wrote this part of the journal, and on what date?

_____

2. What mountains do you think Captain Lewis saw? (Hint: Use the map on page 74.)

_____

3. How were the members of the expedition feeling at this point of the journey?

_____

_____

_____

GO ON ▶

Name _____   Date _____

Part B: Essay ···

Directions   Write a well-developed essay about the Louisiana Purchase and the
Lewis and Clark expedition in the early part of the 1800s. Include an
introduction, supporting paragraphs, and a conclusion. Use the documents
on pages 73–75, your answers to the questions in Part A, and your
knowledge of social studies to help you organize your ideas. Use your
own paper to write the essay.

> **In your essay, remember to discuss:**
>
> • what the Louisiana Purchase was
>
> • why Lewis and Clark went on their expedition
>
> • some of the things the members of the expedition saw
>
> • the hardships and dangers the members of the expedition encountered

Directions   Use the space below to brainstorm. Then write your essay on your
own paper.

Practice Test 2 ···

This practice test is based on documents 1 through 3. It will test your ability to work with historical documents. In Part A, look at each document and answer the question or questions after it. Use your answers to the questions in Part A to help you write your essay in Part B.

Historical Background

During the 1840s, many pioneers began heading west to the new lands explored by Lewis and Clark years earlier. Many of these pioneers followed the Oregon Trail. This trail began in Independence, Missouri. It followed the Platte River to Fort Laramie and then crossed the Rocky Mountains at South Pass. The trail continued through Wyoming and on to the Willamette Valley in Oregon. The pioneers suffered many hardships along the trail, and many of them never reached Oregon.

···

Directions For **Part A**, study EACH document carefully and answer the question or questions after it. These answers will help you write your essay.

For **Part B**, use the information from the documents, your answers from Part A, and your knowledge of social studies to write a well-organized essay. The focus of your essay will be the pioneers traveling the Oregon Trail in the 1840s.

Source: National Archives and Records Administration

Pioneers packed all their belongings in a covered wagon and headed west.

GO ON ▶

Name _____ Date _____

Part A: Short-Answer Questions ·······························

Directions The following documents give information about travel on the Oregon Trail in the 1840s. Study each document carefully. Then answer the question or questions that follow it.

Pioneers used several trails to head west. The map below shows the route of the Oregon Trail. It started in Independence, Missouri, and ended near Portland, Oregon.

Document 1

Trails to the West, 1890

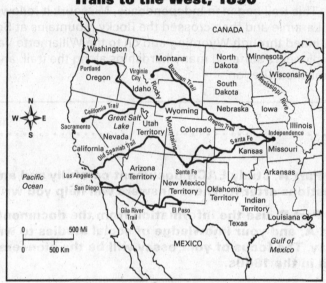

···

Directions Use the map to answer the questions. Write complete sentences.

1. What general direction did pioneers on the Oregon Trail travel?

_____

2. About how far was the journey on the trail from Independence to Portland?

_____

3. Look at the picture of the wagon on page 77. The pioneers usually traveled less than 20 miles a day. About how long do you think the journey from Independence to Oregon would take?

_____

4. Travel then was much different than it is today. What kinds of problems do you think the pioneers might have experienced on their journey?

_____

GO ON ▶

Unit 4: Test Practice with Document-Based Questions
Voices: American History, SV 9781419036385

Name _____ Date _____

Catherine Sager Pringle was a young girl who headed west along the Oregon Trail with her family. Along the way, her leg was crushed, her parents died, and she was later captured by Native Americans.

 Document 2

After Laramie we entered the great American desert, which was hard on the teams. Sickness became common. Father and the boys were all sick. . . . and it soon became apparent that his days were numbered. . . . The evening before his death we crossed Green River and camped on the bank. . . . He said his last hour had come, and his heart was filled with anguish for his family. His wife was ill, the children small, and one likely to be a cripple. They had no relatives near, and a long journey lay before them. . . . Father was buried the next day on the banks of Green River. His coffin was made of two troughs dug out of the body of a tree, but next year emigrants found his bleaching bones, as the Indians had disinterred the remains. . . .

The nights and mornings were very cold, and [Mother] took cold from the exposure unavoidably. With camp fever and a sore mouth, she fought bravely against fate for the sake of her children, but she was taken delirious soon after reaching Fort Bridger, and was bed-fast. . . . We travelled a rough road the day she died, and she moaned fearfully all the time. At night one of the women came in as usual . . . and discovered the pulse was nearly gone. She lived but a few moments, and her last words were, "Oh, Henry! If you only knew how we have suffered." The tent was set up, the corpse laid out, and next morning we took the last look at our mother's face. The grave was near the road; willow brush was laid in the bottom and covered the body, the earth filled in—then the train moved on.

Source: Catherine Sager Pringle, *Across the Plains in 1844*

. . . .

Directions | **Use the journal excerpt to answer the questions. Write complete sentences. Use another sheet of paper.**

1. Catherine Pringle says that her father's "days were numbered." What does she mean by that expression?

2. Near what location did Catherine Pringle's father die?

3. Based upon this short excerpt, how would you characterize Catherine Pringle?

4. Suppose that you are Catherine Pringle. How would you react to the death of the mother?

5. The pioneers knew that their journey would be filled with hardship and death. Why do you think they chose to make the journey anyway?

GO ON ▶

In 1846, a young man named Francis Parkman headed west. He joined a wagon train heading along the Oregon Trail. The next year his journal, *The Oregon Trail: Sketches of Prairie and Rocky-Mountain Life,* was published.

 Document 3

> Shaw and I were much better fitted for this mode of traveling than we had been on betaking ourselves to the prairies for the first time a few months before. The daily routine had ceased to be a novelty. All the details of the journey and the camp had become familiar to us. We had seen life under a new aspect; the human biped had been reduced to his primitive condition. We had lived without law to protect, a roof to shelter, or garment of cloth to cover us. One of us at least had been without bread, and without salt to season his food. Our idea of what is indispensable to human existence and enjoyment had been wonderfully curtailed, and a horse, a rifle, and a knife seemed to make up the whole of life's necessaries. For these once obtained, together with the skill to use them, all else that is essential would follow in their train, and a host of luxuries besides. One other lesson our short prairie experience had taught us; that of profound contentment in the present, and utter contempt for what the future might bring forth.

Source: Francis Parkman, 1847, *The Oregon Trail*, Chapter 20, "The Lonely Journey"

Directions Use the journal excerpt to answer the questions. Write complete sentences. Use another sheet of paper.

1. What things had Parkman been living without on his journey?

2. What three things did Parkman say had become his "life's necessaries"? What are your life's necessities?

3. Parkman says, "the human biped had been reduced to his primitive condition." What does he mean by that statement?

4. Do you think life on the trail was what the pioneers thought it would be? Explain.

5. What do you think life on the trail would be like? Describe a typical day on the trail.

GO ON ▶

Part B: Essay ··

Directions Write a well-developed essay about the pioneers' journey west on the Oregon Trail in the 1840s. Include an introduction, supporting paragraphs, and a conclusion. Use the documents on pages 78–80, your answers to the questions in Part A, and your knowledge of social studies to help you organize your ideas. Use your own paper to write the essay.

> In your essay, remember to discuss:
>
> • the route of the Oregon Trail
>
> • the hardships and dangers of life on the trail
>
> • the kinds of people making the journey and how the trail changed them
>
> • why people would face such troubles to make the journey

···

Directions Use the space below to brainstorm. Then write your essay on your own paper.

Practice Test 3 ····································

Directions This practice test is based on documents 1 through 6. It will test your ability to work with historical documents. In Part A, look at each document and answer the question or questions after it. Consider the context and point of view of each document. Use your answers to the questions in Part A to help you write your essay in Part B.

Historical Background

The period after the Civil War is called Reconstruction. The federal government took steps to help former slaves adjust to new social and economic conditions. These actions met with resistance in Southern states. After President Lincoln's death, "Radical Republicans" in Congress made policy. Laws were passed punishing the South and protecting citizens' rights. In time, public attention turned to other matters, and Reconstruction ended.

··

Directions For **Part A**, study EACH document carefully and answer the question or questions after it. These answers will help you write your essay.

For **Part B**, use the information from the documents, your answers from Part A, and your knowledge of social studies to write a well-organized essay. The focus of your essay will be Reconstruction and its effects.

Celebrating the abolition of slavery in Washington, D.C., dated April 19, 1866

GO ON ▶

Name _____ Date _____

Part A: Short-Answer Questions ·······························

Directions / The following documents show information about the period of Reconstruction in American history. Study each document carefully. Then answer the question or questions that follow it.

The Bureau of Refugees, Freedmen, and Abandoned Lands was established in March 1865. The Freedmen's Bureau, as it was often called, was to provide assistance and education to refugees and freedmen. The Bureau provided food, clothes, and medication for the freed slaves.

Document 1

> The greatest success of the Freedmen's Bureau lay in the planting of the free school among Negroes, and the idea of free elementary education among all classes in the South. It not only called the schoolmistress . . . and built them schoolhouses, but it helped discover and support such apostles of human development as Edmund Ware, Erastus Cravath, and Samuel Armstrong. State superintendents of education were appointed, and by 1870 150,000 children were in school. The opposition to Negro education was bitter in the South, for the South believed an educated Negro to be a dangerous Negro. And the South was not wholly wrong; for education among all kinds of men always has had, and always will have, an element of danger and revolution, of dissatisfaction and discontent. Nevertheless, men strive to know.

Source: "The Freedmen's Bureau" by W.E.B. Du Bois, *Atlantic Monthly*, 1901

· ·

Directions / Write complete sentences to answer the questions.

1. According to the selection, what was the most important thing the Freedmen's Bureau did for the freed slaves?

_____

_____

2. Why were people in the South opposed to educating the freed slaves?

_____

_____

_____

3. Do you agree with the author that education can be a dangerous thing? Explain.

_____

_____

GO ON ▶

After the Civil War, a temporary plan was set up to help some freed slaves. Each freed family was granted forty acres of farming land along the coast of Georgia. Mules that the army no longer needed were also given to settlers. This plan became known as "Forty Acres and a Mule."

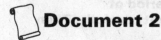 **Document 2**

In the Field, Savannah, Georgia, January 16th, 1865

Special Field Orders, No. 15.

I. The islands from Charleston, south, the abandoned rice fields along the rivers for thirty miles back from the sea, and the country bordering the St. Johns river, Florida, are reserved and set apart for the settlement of the negroes now made free by the acts of war and the proclamation of the President of the United States.

II. At Beaufort, Hilton Head, Savannah, Fernandina, St. Augustine and Jacksonville, the blacks may remain in their chosen or accustomed vocations—but on the islands, and in the settlements hereafter to be established, no white person whatever, unless military officers and soldiers detailed for duty, will be permitted to reside; and the sole and exclusive management of affairs will be left to the freed people themselves, subject only to the United States military authority and the acts of Congress. By the laws of war, and orders of the President of the United States, the negro is free and must be dealt with as such. . . .

—by Order of Major General W. T. Sherman

Source: National Archives and Records Administration

....

Directions Write complete sentences to answer the questions.

1. Why do you think farmland was important to the freed slaves?

_____

_____

2. Why do you think white people were not allowed to live where the freed slaves were granted land?

_____

_____

_____

GO ON ▶

Name _____ Date _____

The Fourteenth Amendment to the Constitution of the United States was ratified on July 9, 1868. It made all persons born in the United States, including freed slaves, citizens of the United States. It also gave due process and equal protection of the laws to all citizens.

 # Document 3

> **Section 1.** All persons born or naturalized in the United States and subject to the jurisdiction thereof, are citizens of the United States and of the State wherein they reside. No State shall make or enforce any law which shall abridge the privileges or immunities of citizens of the United States; nor shall any State deprive any person of life, liberty, or property, without due process of law; nor deny to any person within its jurisdiction the equal protection of the laws.

Source: Fourteenth Amendment to the Constitution of the United States

· ·

Directions / Write complete sentences to answer the questions.

1. Why was it important that the freed slaves were made citizens of the United States?

_____

_____

_____

2. Why is it important that all citizens are protected equally by the laws of the nation?

_____

_____

_____

3. Due process means that people must be tried in courts if they are accused of a crime. Why is due process important?

_____

_____

_____

_____

_____

_____

_____

_____

_____

GO ON ▶

The Fifteenth Amendment was ratified in 1870. It gave African American men the right to vote. However, when the freed slaves tried to vote, they were often threatened.

 Document 4

Source: © Bettmann/CORBIS

A black voter being threatened by white voters who want him to vote against black rights

. . . .

Directions   **Write complete sentences to answer the questions.**

1. In the illustration, what tactics are used to deny freed slaves their rights? (Hint: What are the white voters doing in the illustration?)

_____

_____

_____

2. Do you think all citizens should have the right to vote? Explain.

_____

_____

_____

_____

GO ON ▶

Name _____ Date _____

 Document 5

Congressional Actions (1865–1875)	
Freedmen's Bureau established (1865)	provides relief for the victims of the Civil War finds education, jobs, and homes for freed slaves
The 13th Amendment ratified (1865)	ends slavery
The Reconstruction Act passed (1867)	divides the South into 5 military districts sets guidelines for establishing state governments
The 14th Amendment ratified (1868)	defines citizenship in a way that includes African Americans guarantees all citizens equal protection under the law
The 15th Amendment ratified (1870)	guarantees all male citizens the right to vote gives federal government power to enforce voting rights
The Ku Klux Klan Act passed (1871)	allows federal troops to enforce the 14th Amendment allows government to act against terrorist groups such as the Ku Klux Klan
The Civil Rights Act of 1875 passed	tries to make sure African Americans are treated equally

• •

Directions Write complete sentences to answer the questions.

1. Which amendment gives all citizens equal protection of the laws?

_____

_____

2. What was the purpose of most of these actions by Congress?

_____

_____

_____

3. Which of these Congressional actions do you think would be most helpful in healing the nation after the Civil War? Explain.

_____

_____

_____

_____

4. Read about the three amendments in the chart. Which of these three amendments do you think is the most important?

_____

_____

_____

_____

GO ON ▶

As the years passed, people became less interested in Reconstruction. The administration of President Grant was ineffective, and national concerns turned elsewhere.

Document 6

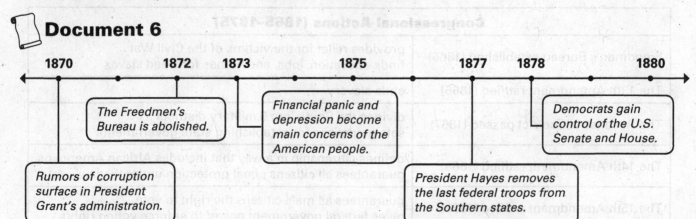

1870   1872   1873   1875   1877   1878   1880

The Freedmen's Bureau is abolished.

Financial panic and depression become main concerns of the American people.

Democrats gain control of the U.S. Senate and House.

Rumors of corruption surface in President Grant's administration.

President Hayes removes the last federal troops from the Southern states.

Directions   **Write complete sentences to answer the questions.**

1. In which year was the Freedmen's Bureau abolished?

_____

2. Which events in 1870 and 1873 lowered interest in Reconstruction? (Hint: Underline in the document the events that occupied the minds of people in the United States.)

_____

_____

3. President Grant and President Hayes were Republicans. What conclusions can you draw from the events of 1877 and 1878?

_____

_____

_____

_____

_____

_____

_____

GO ON ▶

Part B: Essay •••

Directions Write a well-developed essay about federal government goals and policies during Reconstruction and resistance to those efforts in Southern states. Include an introduction, supporting paragraphs, and a conclusion. Use the documents on pages 83–88, your answers to the questions in Part A, and your knowledge of social studies to help you organize your ideas. Use your own paper to write the essay.

In your essay, remember to discuss:

• federal government goals and policies during Reconstruction

• resistance to those efforts in Southern states

• when and why the Reconstruction Era ended

Directions Use the space below to brainstorm. Then write your essay on your own paper.

Practice Test 4 ·······························

Directions This practice test is based on documents 1 through 5. It will test your ability to work with historical documents. In Part A, look at each document and answer the question or questions after it. Use your answers to the questions in Part A to help you write your essay in Part B.

Historical Background

> The United States has been called a "nation of immigrants." Millions of these newcomers first set foot on U.S. soil in New York. The Statue of Liberty stood there to greet them. Their story is one of struggle and triumph.

Directions For **Part A**, study EACH document carefully and answer the question or questions after it. These answers will help you write your essay.

For **Part B**, use the information from the documents, your answers from Part A, and your knowledge of social studies to write a well-organized essay. The focus of your essay will be the immigrants who entered the United States through New York in the 1800s and early 1900s.

GO ON ▶

Name _____   Date _____

Part A: Short-Answer Questions ....

Directions The following documents give information about immigration to the United States in the 1800s and early 1900s. Study each document carefully. Then answer the question or questions that follow it.

In 1883, Emma Lazarus submitted a poem to help raise funds to build a pedestal for a great statue soon to come from France. That statue was built, and it came to be known as the Statue of Liberty. It stands as a symbol of freedom and opportunity. In 1903, Lazarus's poem was cast into a bronze plaque and mounted on an inner wall of the pedestal.

Document 1

The New Colossus

Not like the brazen giant of Greek fame,
With conquering limbs astride from land to land;
Here at our sea-washed, sunset gates shall stand
A mighty woman with a torch, whose flame
Is the imprisoned lightning, and her name
Mother of Exiles. From her beacon-hand
Glows world-wide welcome; her mild eyes command
The air-bridged harbor, that twin cities frame.

"Keep, ancient lands, your storied pomp!" cries she
With silent lips. "Give me your tired, your poor,
Your huddled masses yearning to breathe free,
The wretched refuse of your teeming shore.
Send these, the homeless, tempest-tost to me,
I lift my lamp beside the golden door!"
　　　　　　　—by Emma Lazarus, November 1883

Source: National Park Service

Directions Write complete sentences to answer the questions. Use a separate sheet of paper.

1. In line 11 of the poem, Lazarus writes about "huddled masses yearning to breathe free." What does she mean? Can't the immigrants breathe freely in their own countries?

2. In the last line of the poem, Lazarus uses the golden door as a symbol of the United States. What does she mean by "golden door"?

3. Why would immigrants be attracted to such a golden door?

4. Suppose you were an immigrant in the 1800s. Why would you be attracted to the United States?

GO ON ▶

Name _____ Date _____

In the 1800s, the Industrial Revolution changed economic life in the United States. More workers were needed for new industries that sprang up. There were not enough people living in the United States to fill all the jobs.

 ## Document 2

> Industrious men need never lack employment in America. Laborers, carpenters, masons, bricklayers, stonecutters, tailors, and shoemakers, and the useful mechanics generally are always sure of work and wages. Stonecutters now receive in this city (New York) $2.00 a day, . . . carpenters, $1.87; bricklayers, $2.00; laborers, from $1.00 to $1.25. . . .

Source: *Hints to Emigrants from Europe,* a booklet by the Shamrock Friendly Association of New York City in July 1816

. . . .

Directions **Write complete sentences to answer the questions.**

1. What was one major reason immigrants came to this country in the 1800s?

_____

_____

2. Where would immigrants seeking these opportunities probably settle?

_____

_____

3. What kind of worker do you think you would be if you immigrated to the United States in the 1800s?

_____

_____

GO ON ▶

Name _____   Date _____

Immigrants came to the United States for land, good jobs, and freedom. Thousands and thousands came. The figures in the table below are for selected years between 1892 and 1924. The figures in dark type at the bottom show the totals for the 32 years between 1892 and 1924.

 **Document 3**

Immigration to the United States (1892–1924)		
Year	Through the Port of New York	Total United States
1892	445,987	579,663
1900	341,712	448,572
1907	1,004,756	1,285,349
1914	878,052	1,218,480
1924	315,587	706,896
Total immigrants, 1892–1924	14,277,144*	20,003,041

*71.4% of all immigrants who entered the United States between 1892 and 1924 came through the Port of New York.

Source: U.S. Department of Justice, Immigration and Naturalization Service, Washington, D.C., and *Annual Reports of the Commissioner General of Immigration, 1892–1924*

· ·

Directions | **Write complete sentences to answer the questions.**

1. How many immigrants entered the United States between 1892 and 1924?

_____

2. During which year did the most immigrants enter through the Port of New York?

_____

3. Why was the Port of New York so important to immigration during this period?

_____

_____

_____

_____

_____

_____

GO ON ▶

When the immigrants arrived in the United States, many settled in the poor neighborhoods of New York. They lived in crowded apartment buildings called tenements. Often the tenements were unhealthy or unsafe.

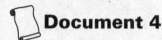

Document 4

Source: *Harper's Weekly* 1883; Library of Congress

Tenement house sufferers on a hot night in New York. Bad conditions for the poor.

For the first year or two they live huddled together in the tenements.

Source: "The Bookworms of New York," *Independent*, January 23, 1913

Directions Write complete sentences to answer the questions.

1. What was life like for many new arrivals in the United States? Give details from the picture to support your answer.

_____

_____

_____

_____

2. Do you think the poor living conditions were what the immigrants dreamed of? Explain.

_____

_____

GO ON ▶

Name _____ Date _____

Document 5

> In each of these [neighborhoods] there is a public library—so placed, not by design, but by accident. Their readers once were mostly of one nationality. Now various peoples read in all of them. In the evening the men who work in the stores, the factories, on the docks, or streets, come to the library for the books. Those who have families carry home the volumes as paternally as they lug food or clothing—perhaps more so if they happen to be very poor . . . most of them are spurred by a desire for leadership and they are picking education as a path to the goal.

Source: "The Bookworms of New York," *Independent*, January 23, 1913

Directions Write complete sentences to answer the questions.

1. Why do you think the immigrants went to the libraries?

_____

_____

_____

2. Why do you think a poor immigrant might carry a book so carefully?

_____

_____

_____

3. How did libraries improve immigrants' lives and futures?

_____

_____

_____

GO ON ▶

Part B: Essay ···

Directions Write a well-developed essay about U.S. immigrants' lives in the 1800s and early 1900s. Include an introduction, supporting paragraphs, and a conclusion. Use the documents on pages 91–95, your answers to the questions in Part A, and your knowledge of social studies to help you organize your ideas. Use your own paper to write the essay.

In your essay, remember to discuss:

• why and how immigrants came to the United States

• what immigrants did after they arrived

• what the lives of many immigrants were like at first

• the efforts immigrants made to succeed

···

Directions Use the space below to brainstorm. Then write your essay on your own paper.

Practice Test 5 ···

Directions | This practice test is based on documents 1 through 6. It will test your ability to work with historical documents. In Part A, look at each document and answer the question or questions after it. Consider the context and point of view of each document. Use your answers to the questions in Part A to help you write your essay in Part B.

Historical Background

> Throughout the 1920s, stock prices continued to climb. The apparent prosperity, however, was an illusion. In October 1929, the stock market crashed. This financial disaster plunged the economy of the United States into turmoil. The period of suffering and despair that followed the crash is known as the Great Depression.

Source: National Archives and Records Administration

Unemployed men in a breadline at an Al Capone soup kitchen, Chicago, 1931

GO ON ▶

Name _____ Date _____

Part A: Short-Answer Questions ·····························

Directions The following documents show information about the Great Depression in the 1930s and its effect on the United States. Study each document carefully. Then answer the question or questions that follow it.

Document 1

> They are the people who our post offices label "address unknown." . . . Every group in society is represented in their ranks, from the college graduate to the child who has never seen the inside of the schoolhouse. Expectant mothers, sick babies, young childless couples, grim-faced middle-aged [who lost] lifetime jobs—[homeless]. We think of nomads of the desert—now we have nomads of the Depression.

Source: Newton D. Baker, writing in *The New York Times* in 1932 (quoted in *The Glory and the Dream* by William Manchester)

···

Directions Write complete sentences to answer the questions.

1. Who was affected by the Great Depression?

_____

_____

_____

2. How were these groups affected?

_____

_____

_____

3. What is a nomad? Who were the "nomads of the Depression" the author identifies?

_____

_____

_____

_____

_____

GO ON ▶

Document 2

> We lost everything. It was the time I would collect four, five hundred dollars a week. After that, I couldn't collect fifteen, ten dollars a week. I was going around trying to collect enough money to keep my family going. Very few people could pay you. Maybe a dollar if they would feel sorry for you or what.
>
> We tried to struggle along living day by day. Then I couldn't pay the rent. I had a little car, but I couldn't pay no license for it. I left it parked against the court. I sold it for $15 in order to buy some food for the family. I had three little children. It was a time when I didn't even have money to buy a pack of cigarettes, and I was a smoker. I didn't have a nickel in my pocket.
>
> Finally people started to talk me into going into the relief. They had open soup kitchens. Al Capone, he had open soup kitchens somewhere downtown, where people were standing in line. And you had to go two blocks, stand there, around the corner, to get a bowl of soup. . . .
>
> I didn't want to go on relief. Believe me, when I was forced to go to the office of the relief, the tears were running out of my eyes. I couldn't bear myself to take money from anybody for nothing. If it wasn't for those kids . . . many a time it came to my mind to go commit suicide. . . .

Source: Ben Isaacs, clothing salesman, from *Hard Times: An Oral History of the Great Depression*
Reprinted by permission of Donadio & Olson, Inc. Copyright © 1970 by Studs Terkel.

· ·

Directions **Write complete sentences to answer the questions.**

1. What happened to Ben Isaacs's family when the Great Depression started?

_____

_____

_____

2. What did Ben Isaacs have to do to support his family during the Great Depression?

_____

_____

_____

_____

_____

_____

_____

GO ON ▶

Name _____ Date _____

Document 3

> The Depression is over.

President Herbert Hoover in 1930

Document 4

> After the Great Crash came the Great Depression which lasted . . . for ten years. In 1933, Gross National Product (total production of the economy) was nearly a third less than in 1929. . . . Between 1930 and 1940 only once, in 1937, did the average number unemployed during the year drop below eight million. In 1933 nearly thirteen million were out of work, or about one in every four in the labor force. In 1938 one person in five was still out of work. . . .

Source: *The Great Crash: 1929* by John Kenneth Galbraith

• •

Directions Write complete sentences to answer the questions.

1. According to Document 4, what were two effects of the Great Depression?

_____

_____

_____

_____

2. Based on Hoover's statement in Document 3, do you think his understanding of the severity of the Great Depression was realistic? Explain using evidence from Document 4.

_____

_____

_____

_____

_____

_____

_____

GO ON ▶

Franklin Delano Roosevelt was elected the new president in 1932. In March of the next year, he offered hope to the nation in his inaugural address.

Document 5

> In such a spirit on my part and on yours we face our common difficulties. They concern, thank God, only material things. Values have shrunken to fantastic levels; taxes have risen; our ability to pay has fallen; government of all kinds is faced by serious curtailment of income; the means of exchange are frozen in the currents of trade; the withered leaves of industrial enterprise lie on every side; farmers find no markets for their produce; the savings of many years in thousands of families are gone.
>
> More important, a host of unemployed citizens face the grim problem of existence, and an equally great number toil with little return. Only a foolish optimist can deny the dark realities of the moment. . . .
>
> Our greatest primary task is to put people to work. This is no unsolvable problem if we face it wisely and courageously. It can be accomplished in part by direct recruiting by the Government itself, treating the task as we would treat the emergency of a war, but at the same time, through this employment, accomplishing greatly needed projects to stimulate and reorganize the use of our natural resources.

Source: Franklin D. Roosevelt inaugural address, March 1933

• •

Directions | **Write complete sentences to answer the questions.**

1. Summarize the problems President Roosevelt described in his speech.

_____

_____

_____

2. What did President Roosevelt say was the nation's most important task?

_____

_____

3. President Roosevelt's plan was for the government to provide jobs. What would these new government jobs do?

_____

_____

_____

GO ON ▶

Name _____ Date _____

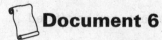

Labor Force, Employment, and Unemployment in the United States, 1929–1941 (Millions of Persons)				
			Unemployment	
Year	Labor Force	Employed	Number	Percent of Labor Force
1929	49,180	47,630	1,550	3.2
1930	49,820	45,480	4,340	8.7
1931	50,420	42,400	8,020	15.9
1932	51,000	38,940	12,060	23.6
1933	51,590	38,760	12,830	24.9
1934	52,230	40,890	11,340	21.7
1935	52,870	42,260	10,610	20.1
1936	53,440	44,410	9,030	16.9
1937	54,000	46,300	7,700	14.3
1938	54,610	44,220	10,390	19.0
1939	55,230	45,750	9,480	17.2
1940	55,640	47,520	8,120	14.6
1941	55,910	50,350	5,560	9.9

Source: U.S. Bureau of the Census, 1960

Directions Write complete sentences to answer the questions.

1. In which year were the most people in the United States unemployed? What percent of the labor force was unemployed that year?

_____

_____

_____

2. How successful were the programs President Roosevelt started in solving the unemployment problem? Use information from the chart to support your answer.

_____

_____

_____

GO ON ▶

Name _____ Date _____

Part B: Essay ....

Directions Write a well-developed essay about the Great Depression. Include an introduction, supporting paragraphs, and a conclusion. Use the documents on pages 98–102, your answers to the questions in Part A, and your knowledge of social studies to help you organize your ideas. Use your own paper to write the essay.

In your essay, remember to:

- discuss two effects of the Great Depression on the people of the United States
- explain two actions taken to solve the problems of the Depression
- evaluate the success of the approach taken by President Roosevelt

Directions Use the space below to brainstorm. Then write your essay on your own paper.

Name _____ Date _____

Practice Test 6 ···

Directions This practice test is based on documents 1 through 3. It will test your ability to work with historical documents. In Part A, look at each document and answer the question or questions after it. Consider the context and point of view of each document. Use your answers to the questions in Part A to help you write your essay in Part B.

Historical Background

In the 1930s, great dust storms in the Midwest combined with economic woes to create hard times for farmers. The dust storms were so thick that visibility was often zero and dust seeped into everything. The storms were the result of years of drought and farmland that had been overplanted. The drought started in 1930, and by 1934, the Great Plains had become a desert known as the Dust Bowl. Houses and the landscape were soon buried in dust. You can see the effects of the dust storms in the photograph below. The picture was taken by Arthur Rothstein in 1936.

Source: National Archives and Records Administration

Farmer and sons walking in the face of a dust storm, Cimarron County, Oklahoma

GO ON ▶

Name _____ Date _____

Part A: Short-Answer Questions ·····················

Directions The following documents show information about the Dust Bowl in the 1930s. Study each document carefully. Then answer the question or questions that follow it.

To escape the Dust Bowl, many families just packed up and headed west. Many went to California to find a better life. The map below shows some of the routes out of the Dust Bowl. One of the most popular was Highway 66, often called Route 66.

Document 1

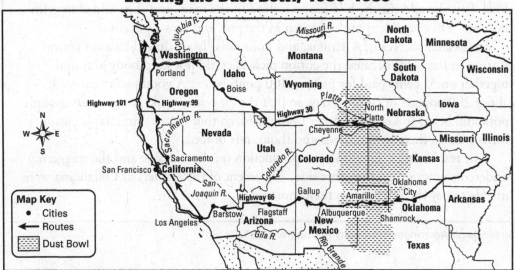

Leaving the Dust Bowl, 1930–1939

Directions Use the map to answer the questions.

1. In which general direction did the people leaving the Dust Bowl travel?

_____

2. Which route ran from North Platte, Nebraska, to Portland, Oregon? Which other historical route ran this way? (Hint: Look back at the map on page 78.)

_____

3. Which route ran from Amarillo, Texas, to Barstow, California?

_____

4. Name a state that was part of the Dust Bowl.

_____

_____

GO ON ▶

Name _____ Date _____

In 1932, Oscar Ameringer, a newspaper editor from Oklahoma, gave testimony to a Congressional committee on unemployment and the plight of farmers. He described common problems in the Dust Bowl. By 1932, almost 25 percent of people in the United States were out of work, and farmers could not sell their crops for enough to pay their mortgages.

 Document 2

The roads of the West and Southwest teem with hungry hitchhikers. The campfires of the homeless are seen along every railroad track. I saw men, women, and children walking over the hard roads. Most of them were tenant farmers who had lost their all in the late slump in wheat and cotton. Between Clarksville and Russellville, Arkansas, I picked up a family. The woman was hugging a dead chicken under a ragged coat. When I asked her where she had procured the fowl, first she told me she had found it dead in the road, and then added in grim humor, "They promised me a chicken in the pot, and now I got mine."

In Oklahoma, Texas, Arkansas, and Louisiana, I saw untold bales of cotton rotting in the fields because the cotton pickers could not keep body and soul together on 35 cents paid for picking 100 pounds. . . . A good picker can pick about 200 pounds of cotton a day, so that the 70 cents would not provide enough pork and beans to keep the picker in the field, so that there is fine staple cotton rotting down there by hundreds and thousands of tons.

As a result of this appalling overproduction on the one side and the staggering underconsumption on the other side, 70 percent of the farmers of Oklahoma were unable to pay the interests on their mortgages.

Source: Oscar Ameringer, testimony to Congress, 1932

. . . .

Directions / **Use Oscar Ameringer's testimony to answer the questions.**

1. How much would a worker make for picking 100 pounds of cotton? _____

2. Who did Ameringer say most of the hungry hitchhikers were? _____

_____

3. What caused many of the Oklahoma farmers to be unable to pay their mortgages?

_____

_____

_____

_____

_____

GO ON ▶

106
Unit 4: Test Practice with Document-Based Questions
Voices: American History, SV 9781419036385

Name _____ Date _____

Many of the farmers who lost their homes packed up all their belongings and headed west. The photograph below shows one such family.

Document 3

Source: National Archives and Records Administration

Farmers who lost their farms joined the caravans of "Okies" on Route 66 to California, 1935

Directions   **Use the photograph to answer the questions. Write complete sentences. Use another sheet of paper.**

1. Route 66 was a major highway in the 1930s. How does it compare to modern highways?

2. Did this family have many possessions? How can you tell?

3. Which other group of people you have read about also packed up their belongings and headed west?

4. Look back at the map on page 105. Which highway on the map took a route similar to the Oregon Trail?

5. Imagine that you lost your home and had to leave for an unfamiliar place. How do you think you would feel?

GO ON ▶

Part B: Essay

Directions Write a well-developed essay about the Dust Bowl. Include an introduction, supporting paragraphs, and a conclusion. Use the documents on pages 105–107, your answers to the questions in Part A, and your knowledge of social studies to help you organize your ideas. Use your own paper to write the essay.

> **In your essay, remember to discuss:**
>
> • the cause of the Dust Bowl
>
> • the effect of the drought and dust storms on families in the Midwest
>
> • what the families did to escape the Dust Bowl

Directions Use the space below to brainstorm. Then write your essay on your own paper.

Name _____ Date _____

Practice Test 7 ···

Directions This practice test is based on documents 1 through 7. It will test your ability to work with historical documents. In Part A, look at each document and answer the question or questions after it. Consider the context and point of view of each document. Use your answers to the questions in Part A to help you write your essay in Part B.

Historical Background

In the 1930s, Adolf Hitler and his National Socialist Party, or Nazis, came to power in Germany. In 1939, Germany invaded Poland, and World War II began. The United States did not enter the war until Japan attacked Pearl Harbor, Hawaii, on December 7, 1941. After much fighting and loss of life in Europe and the Pacific, World War II ended in August 1945.

Source: National Archives and Records Administration

The battleship *Arizona* burns after the Japanese attack on Pearl Harbor, December 1941.

GO ON ▶

www.harcourtschoolsupply.com
© Harcourt Achieve Inc. All rights reserved

109

Unit 4: Test Practice with Document-Based Questions
Voices: American History, SV 9781419036385

Part A: Short-Answer Questions ·····················

Directions The following documents show information about World War II. Study each document carefully. Then answer the question or questions that follow it.

Source: National Archives and Records Administration

President Franklin D. Roosevelt

On December 8, 1941, President Franklin Roosevelt, or FDR, went before Congress to request a declaration of war against Japan. The request was overwhelmingly approved, and the United States entered World War II against Japan and later against Germany.

Document 1

> Yesterday, December 7, 1941—a date which will live in infamy—the United States of America was suddenly and deliberately attacked by naval and air forces of the Empire of Japan. The United States was at peace with that nation. . . .
>
> The attack yesterday on the Hawaiian Islands has caused severe damage to American naval and military forces. Very many American lives have been lost. In addition American ships have been reported torpedoed on the high seas between San Francisco and Honolulu. . . .
>
> Hostilities exist. There is no blinking at the fact that our people, our territory, and our interests are in grave danger. . . .
>
> I ask that the Congress declare that since the unprovoked and dastardly attack by Japan on Sunday, December 7, a state of war has existed between the United States and the Japanese Empire.

Source: President Franklin D. Roosevelt, address to Congress, December 8, 1941

··

Directions Use President Roosevelt's speech to answer the questions. Write complete sentences. Use another sheet of paper.

1. Why did President Roosevelt ask Congress to declare war against Japan?

2. What did Roosevelt mean when he spoke of "a date which will live in infamy"?

3. Do you think President Roosevelt was right to take the nation to war against Japan? Explain your opinion.

GO ON ▶

Name _____   Date _____

World War II began in September 1939 when Germany invaded Poland. Within days, Europe was in a state of war. The United States remained neutral until the Japanese attack on Pearl Harbor in December 1941. After that, the United States joined the Allies to battle the Axis forces of Germany, Italy, and Japan. The war ended in Europe in May 1945. After the United States dropped atomic bombs on Hiroshima and Nagasaki, Japan surrendered. The war in the Pacific ended in August 1945.

Document 2

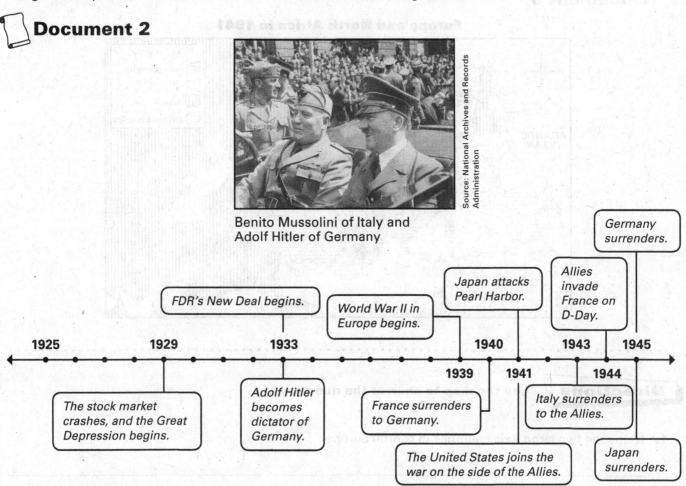

Benito Mussolini of Italy and
Adolf Hitler of Germany

Source: National Archives and Records Administration

Germany surrenders.

Allies invade France on D-Day.

Japan attacks Pearl Harbor.

FDR's New Deal begins.

World War II in Europe begins.

| 1925 | 1929 | 1933 | | 1940 | 1943 | 1945 |

1939   1941   1944

The stock market crashes, and the Great Depression begins.

Adolf Hitler becomes dictator of Germany.

France surrenders to Germany.

Italy surrenders to the Allies.

The United States joins the war on the side of the Allies.

Japan surrenders.

Directions   Use the time line to answer the questions. Write complete sentences.

1. Who became the dictator of Germany in 1933?

_____

2. What place did Japan attack on December 7, 1941?

_____

3. On June 6, 1944, thousands of Allied soldiers invaded France. What name was given to that day?

_____

4. In what year did Germany and Japan surrender to end World War II?

_____

GO ON ▶

A world war involves fighting around the globe. The maps on this page and on page 113 show how few parts of the world remained untouched by conflict. As shown on the map below, many of the countries that fell to the Axis forces were on the side of the Allies.

Document 3

Europe and North Africa in 1941

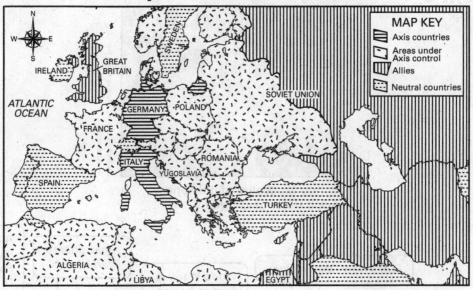

MAP KEY
- Axis countries
- Areas under Axis control
- Allies
- Neutral countries

Directions Use the map to answer the questions.

1. Name the two large Axis countries in central Europe.

_____

2. Based on the map, which side—Axis or Allies—seemed to be winning the war in 1941? Explain.

_____

_____

3. Circle a neutral country on the map. Why do you think that country did not pick sides when fighting was going on all around?

_____

_____

_____

_____

_____

GO ON ▶

Name _____ Date _____

The map below shows some of the battles in the Pacific front of World War II. Many of the battles took place on small islands in the Pacific Ocean.

 Document 4

World War II in the Pacific

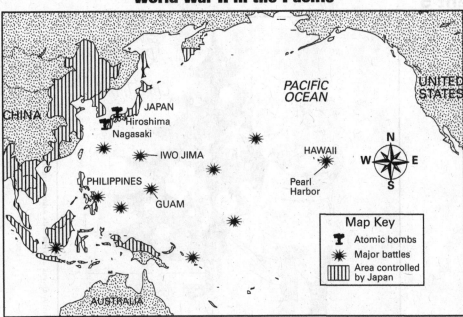

· ·

Directions   Use the map to answer the questions.

1. Where is Pearl Harbor located? _____

2. Name two islands in the Pacific where battles took place.

_____

3. The United States dropped atomic bombs on two cities in Japan. Name those two cities.

_____

4. Why do you think the mainland of the United States was not the scene of any battles?

_____

_____

_____

_____

_____

Name _____ Date _____

During World War II, the nation rallied to support the war effort. One way to support the cause was to buy war bonds. War bonds were used to finance the war and as a kind of savings. Like savings bonds, war bonds paid interest. Many different posters urging citizens to buy war bonds were created. The one shown below was drawn by Charles Alston in 1943.

 ## Document 5

· ·

Directions | Use the poster to answer the questions. Write complete sentences.

1. What gift is Santa delivering?

_____

2. Why do you think Santa is wearing a helmet?

_____

_____

3. Why do you think a war bond is called "the best present for the best future"?

_____

_____

_____

_____

GO ON ▶

During the war, many women in the United States entered the workplace. They did the jobs necessary to support the soldiers overseas. These women were symbolized by a character called Rosie the Riveter. She is shown in the poster below. The poster was drawn by J. Howard Miller in 1942.

 Document 6

Source: National Archives and Records Administration

. . . .

Directions Use the poster to answer the questions. Write complete sentences.

1. Why did women in the United States enter the workplace? Why didn't men do the jobs?

_____

_____

2. Why is the woman in the poster showing her muscle?

_____

_____

3. Why do you think women were willing to take an active part in the war effort?

_____

_____

_____

GO ON ▶

The war in Europe ended in May 1945, but the war in the Pacific dragged on. At last President Truman decided to drop a new kind of bomb on a Japanese city. On August 6, 1945, an atomic bomb was dropped on Hiroshima. Nearly 100,000 people were killed instantly, but still Japan did not surrender. On August 9, 1945, a second atomic bomb was dropped on Nagasaki. This time, about 70,000 residents were killed instantly. After this second bombing, Japan surrendered to end World War II.

Document 7

Source: National Archives and Records Administration

A plume of smoke rises after the bombing of Nagasaki, August 9, 1945.

· ·

Directions Use the photograph to answer the questions. Write complete sentences.

1. This photograph shows the great destructive force of the atomic bomb. How does the photograph make you feel?

_____

_____

2. President Truman was worried that the war would drag on and thousands more U.S. soldiers would die. So he decided to drop the atomic bombs on Hiroshima and Nagasaki. Do you think he made the correct decision? Explain.

_____

_____

_____

GO ON ▶

Name _____ Date _____

Part B: Essay ···

Directions | Write a well-developed essay about World War II. Include an introduction, supporting paragraphs, and a conclusion. Use the documents on pages 110–116, your answers to the questions in Part A, and your knowledge of social studies to help you organize your ideas. Use your own paper to write the essay.

> **In your essay, remember to discuss:**
>
> • when, how, and why World War II started
>
> • when and why the United States entered the war
>
> • where most of the fighting took place
>
> • how U.S. citizens were involved in the war effort
>
> • when and how World War II ended

···

Directions | Use the space below to brainstorm. Then write your essay on your own paper.

Name _____   Date _____

Written Document Worksheet

OBSERVATION

Type of Document (Check one):

☐ Excerpt from Book or Magazine   ☐ Letter   ☐ Press Release

☐ Newspaper   ☐ Telegram   ☐ Memorandum

☐ Speech   ☐ Government Document   ☐ Report

☐ Advertisement   ☐ Congressional Record or Testimony   ☐ Other

Date of Document

Author or Creator of the Document

INTERPRETATION

List three important details or facts from the document.

_____

_____

What is the purpose of the document? Why do you think this document was written?

What evidence in the document helps you understand the purpose? Use quotes from the document.

Who is the target audience of the document?

List two things the document tells about life in the United States at the time it was written.

_____

_____

Write a brief summary of the document.

QUESTIONS

Are there any questions you have not had answered by the document?

Where could you find answers to these questions?

Name _____ Date _____

Map Worksheet

OBSERVATION

Type of Map (Check one or more):

☐ Political Map   ☐ Region Map   ☐ Weather Map

☐ Historical Map   ☐ Resource Map   ☐ Events or Attractions Map

☐ Population Map   ☐ Landform Map   ☐ Elevation Map

☐ Route or Highway Map   ☐ Rivers or Waterways Map   ☐ Other

Unique Features of the Map (Check one or more):

☐ Title   ☐ Legend (key)   ☐ Latitude-Longitude Grid

☐ Compass Rose   ☐ Distance Scale   ☐ Other

Date of the Map

INTERPRETATION

List three details in this map you think are important.

_____

_____

_____

What is the purpose of the map? Why do you think the map was drawn?

What evidence in the map helps you understand the purpose?

Does the information in this map support or not support information that you have read? Explain.

QUESTIONS

Are there any questions you have not had answered by the map?

Name _____ Date _____

Photograph Worksheet

OBSERVATION

Study the photograph for two minutes. Form an overall impression of the photograph, and then examine individual items. Next, divide the photo into four equal sections and study each section to see what new details become visible.

Use the chart to list people, objects, and events in the photograph.

People	Objects	Events

INTERPRETATION

Based on what you have observed, list three things you can conclude from this photograph.

_____

_____

_____

How does the photograph affect you or make you feel?

QUESTIONS

What questions does this photograph raise for you?

Where could you find answers to these questions?

Name _____ Date _____

Poster Worksheet

OBSERVATION

What is the main image or words on the poster?

What are the main colors used in the poster?

Are the messages in the poster primarily visual, verbal, or both?

Who created the poster?

When was the poster created?

INTERPRETATION

What symbols (if any) are used in the poster?

If a symbol is used, is it easy to understand, memorable, or dramatic?

What is the main message of the poster?

Who do you think is the target audience for the poster?

What does the poster try to make the audience do?

If the poster was created by the government, what government purpose is served by the poster?

Effective posters use images or symbols that are bold, simple, and direct. Is this an effective poster?

QUESTIONS

What questions do you have about the poster?

How would you have drawn the poster differently?

Name _____ Date _____

Political Cartoon Worksheet

OBSERVATION

List the objects or people in the cartoon.

Identify the cartoon caption or title.

Record any important dates or numbers in the cartoon.

Describe the action taking place in the cartoon.

INTERPRETATION

Are any of the people or objects in your list labeled? What do those labels mean?

Are any of the people or objects in your list symbols? What do they represent?

Which words or phrases in the cartoon are the most important? Explain.

List adjectives that describe emotions portrayed in the cartoon.

What is the message of the cartoon?

Is the cartoon effective in presenting its message?

Which special-interest groups might agree or disagree with the cartoon's message? Why?

QUESTIONS

What questions do you have about the cartoon?

How would you have drawn the cartoon differently?

Answer Key ··

Page 9
Answers will vary.
Accept any reasonable
responses.
1. to create a unified
nation
2. maintain order within
the nation
3. gain freedom

Page 10
1. $2,025,218,000,000
2. 1990 to 2000
3. 1950

Page 11
1. C
2. A
3. C
4. D
5. B
6. A

Page 12
1. C
2. D
3. A
4. C

Page 13
1. B
2. B

Page 14
1. The Contiguous
United States of
America
2. state capital
3.–5. Answers will vary.

Page 15
1. Union
2. California or Oregon
3. Union
4. South
5. territories

Page 16
1. Abraham Lincoln
2. Andrew Johnson
3. governor
4. Answers will vary.

Page 17
1. February 23, 1945

2. soldiers raising the
U.S. flag
3. Answers will vary.

Page 18
1. outside the fence
2. that Bryan would
probably never be
president

Page 19
1. September 22, 1776
2. He seems brave and
patriotic.
3. Answers will vary.

Page 21
1. D
2. C
3. C
4. A
5.–8. Answers will vary.
5. Lincoln was trying to
inspire the crowd to
fight for freedom.
6. Lincoln means that the
soldiers died for their
cause.
7. Lincoln says the
soldiers fought to save
the nation.
8. Lincoln says the
crowd should honor
the fallen soldiers and
take up their cause.

Page 22
1. The plane flew 852
feet in 59 seconds.
2. Answers will vary.
3. Answers will vary.

Page 23
1.–2., 4. Answers will
vary but should show
an understanding of
the documents.
3. Airplanes today are
bigger and faster, and
they have a different
shape and a different
kind of engine.

Page 24
1. B
2. C
3. B
4. A
5. Answers will vary
but will probably
suggest the North was
stronger.
6. Answers will vary but
will probably suggest
the North should win.

Page 25
1. The cold war ended in
1991.
2. The United States
became the strongest
world leader.
3. The United States
began a war on
terrorism.
4. Answers will vary.

Page 26
1. D
2. B
3. B
4. C
5. Answers will vary.

Page 27
1. About two million
people were in unions.
2. Union membership
dropped between
1920 and 1930.
3. From 1930 to 1980,
the number of union
members increased.
4. From 1980 to 2000,
the number of union
members decreased.
5. Answers will vary but
might suggest that
the decrease in union
membership means
there is less interest in
joining unions.

Page 28
1. There were 474,559
more Union soldiers
than Confederate
soldiers.

2. Answers may vary.
The North had a
stronger economy, a
greater population,
and more soldiers.
3. Answers will vary
but should show a
knowledge of both
documents.

Page 29
1. Most immigrants to
the United States
in 1900 came from
Europe.
2. Most immigrants to
the United States in
1990 came from Latin
America.
3. Answers will vary
but might suggest
that Latin America is
closer to the United
States and in worse
economic shape than
Europe.
4. Answers will vary.

Page 30
1. Rhode Island,
Connecticut,
Massachusetts, or
New Hampshire
2. Appalachian
Mountains
3. south
4. France
5. Answers will vary but
should show some
awareness of history.

Page 31
Students should circle
named parts of the map.
1. farming
2. Answers will vary but
should be shown on
map.
3. hunting and gathering,
fishing
4. southeast
5. farming, hunting and
gathering, and some
fishing

6. Answers will vary but should suggest the colonists had the same food sources as the Native Americans in that area.

Page 32
Answers will vary. One boy in the photograph is missing a leg.

Page 33
1. The central image is a young serviceman and a young woman kissing.
2. Answers will vary. The other people seem surprised or happy. After all, the war has just ended.
3. Answers will vary.

Page 34
1. The poster is trying to get people to enlist in the U.S. Army.
2. The target audience is probably young men.
3. The man in the poster is known as Uncle Sam. He represents the United States.
4. Answers may vary. The poster is mostly visual. The picture of the man takes up two-thirds of the poster, and the pointing finger commands the viewer's eye.

Page 35
1. They are not satisfied because the candidate has made only empty compliments to the crowd.
2. No, he says only nice things about the people and the town.
3. Answers may vary. The main idea is that political candidates are often full of hot air and empty promises.
4. Answers will vary.

Page 36
1. The fence represents the border between the United States and Mexico.
2. The man jumping the fence is known as Uncle Sam. He represents the United States.
3. Answers will vary. Yes, the town in the background is burning, and Villa has a burning torch in his hand.

Page 37
1. Unalienable rights, often called inalienable rights, are rights that cannot be taken from a person.
2. The three unalienable rights mentioned in the Declaration of Independence are life, liberty, and the pursuit of happiness.
3. Answers will vary.

Page 38
1. Answers will vary but might include *gale, resounding, brethren,* and *idle.*
2. He means that the next time the wind blows, or soon, they will be at war.
3. His main idea is to give him liberty or give him death.
4.–5. Answers will vary.

Page 39
1. Dr. Stone presented his testimony on May 16, 1865.
2.–4. Answers will vary.

Page 40
Answers will vary. Be sure the students address the questions asked.

Page 41
1. Baum thinks the military leaders are weak and incompetent.
2. His solution is to kill all the Indians.
3. Answers will vary but may include his call to exterminate the Indians and his uncomplimentary names for them.
4. Answers will vary.
5. Answers will vary but should directly address the question.

Page 42
Answers will vary but should directly address the questions.

Page 43
1. B
2. A
3. B
4. C

Page 44
1. Women in every state were finally allowed to vote in 1920.
2. The stock market crashed, and millions of people lost their jobs. In response, Roosevelt's New Deal created jobs.
3.–4. Answers will vary.

Page 45
1. B
2. D
3. B
4. D
5. Answers will vary.

Page 46
1. Parliament passed the Stamp Act in 1765.
2. The Boston Tea Party occurred in 1773.
3. Three battles occurred in 1775.
4. Answers will vary.

Page 47
1. The most U.S. soldiers were in Vietnam in 1968.
2. From 1965 to 1968, the number of U.S. soldiers in Vietnam increased.
3. From 1968 to 1972, the number of U.S. soldiers in Vietnam decreased.
4. Answers will vary.

Page 48
Answers may vary.
1. The United States produced about 7 million barrels of oil per day in 1960.
2. The United States produced just over 7 million barrels of oil per day in 1990.
3. Though oil production peaked in the 1970s and the mid-1980s, the oil production in 1960 and 1990 was about the same.
4. The United States used about 10 million barrels of oil per day in 1960.
5. The United States used about 17 million barrels of oil per day in 1990.
6. Oil usage in the United States leveled off between 1980 and 1990.
7. Oil production and usage were not in balance between 1960 and 1990. The United States used much more oil than it produced.

Page 49
1. Idaho, Utah, Wyoming, or Colorado
2. the eastern half
3. Answers will vary but may suggest that

many of the women in the West were the pioneer women and girls who had gone west in the mid-1800s. Life in the West was different from life in the East, so their ideas may have been different, too.

Page 50
1. central part
2. the Sioux reservation
3. about 40°N and 110°W

Page 51
1. C
2. D
3. First, farmers planted wheat, which destroyed the prairie grasses that held the soil in place. Then, seven years of drought left the soil dry and loose. Wind storms blew dust off the dry fields, and everything in the area was coated with dust.
4. To prevent another dust bowl, people have planted thousands of trees to hold down the soil and block the wind on the Great Plains.
5. Answers will vary.

Page 52
1. The target audience of the poster seems to be young men.
2. The main words on the poster are *man, join,* and *navy.* They convey the main idea of the poster.
3. The main idea is that young men should join the navy.
4. Answers will vary, but young men are often attracted to young women.

Page 53
1. The words try to stir the reader's emotions.
2. The persuasive appeal of the poster is mostly emotional. The poster tries to scare people and make them angry.
3.–4. Answers will vary.

Page 54
1. The photograph was taken in Washington, D.C., on August 28, 1963.
2. The crowd seems to be large.
3. Answers will vary.

Page 55
1. Answers will vary but may suggest the leaders were both black and white.
2. Answers will vary but may suggest that Lincoln also believed in freedom and civil rights.

Page 56
1. A lobbyist is pouring money into the politician's pocket. Answers will vary but may suggest that the lobbyist is trying to win favor with the politician.
2. The people with signs are regular citizens. The fence cuts them off from easy access to the politician. In this case, the fence might represent a lack of money or influence.
3. "Pork barrel" legislation deals with money designated for a politician's special projects back home.
4. Answers will vary.
5. The main idea of the cartoon is that political decisions are often based on

contributions to the politicians.

Page 57
1. The cartoon was first published on May 18, 1948.
2. The two men represent Congress and the president.
3. The fence represents the separation of powers in the U.S. government.
4. Congress is interfering with the executive branch, so the chief executive of the nation wants to maintain the separation of powers.
5. It keeps the government in balance by not allowing any one branch to become too strong.

Page 58
1. The photograph shows that many buildings were destroyed by the earthquake.

Page 59
Answers will vary. Students should indicate the descriptive images in London's report.

Page 60
1. On April 18, Paul Revere and William Dawes rode across the countryside warning the American colonists of the advance of the British Army.
2. The battles of Concord and Lexington occurred the following day, April 19.
3. Soon after Washington was made commander in chief, a battle took place at Bunker Hill.
4. Answers will vary.

Page 61
1. Students should circle the battle sites at Concord, Lexington, and Bunker Hill.
2. Concord and Lexington are about six miles apart.
3. The two hills are about one mile apart.
4. According to the map, Paul Revere rode about 12 miles.
5. Answers will vary.

Page 62
Answers will vary but should directly mention the documents.

Page 64
1. Ships from New England carried goods to Africa.
2. The traders from New England received African people (to be sold as slaves) in exchange for their cargo.
3. The slaves were taken to the West Indies.

Page 65
1. Almost all slaves, in both 1790 and 1820, were in the Southern states.
2. Between 1790 and 1820, the enslaved population decreased in the New England states and the Middle Atlantic states.
3. Between 1790 and 1820, the enslaved population almost doubled in the Southern states.

Page 66
1. The slaves are working in a cotton field.
2. Answers will vary but should use evidence of hard work from the picture.
3. Answers will vary.

Page 67
1. The reward for Nat was $25.
2. Slavery destroyed relationships between parents and children and between husbands and wives. Students should use examples from the advertisements.

Page 68
1. *The Liberator* was first published in 1831.
2. The antislavery movement was getting stronger, from protests in the late 1700s to the creation of a society to fight against slavery in 1833.

Page 69
1. Most of the free states were in the North and the West.
2. Most of the slave states were in the South.
3. Answers will vary.
4. The opponents of slavery wanted to limit it if they could not stop it. If the new territories became slave states, then the problem of slavery might get even worse.

Page 73
1. Captain William Clark wrote this part of the journal on May 23, 1804.
2. The journal suggests the expedition members hunted for much of their food.
3. Two dangers noted in the journal were swift currents in the water and the possibility of falling off landforms.

Page 74
1. St. Louis
2. north and west
3. The size doubled.
4. West of the Mississippi River

Page 75
1. Captain Meriwether Lewis wrote this part of the journal on August 12, 1805.
2. Captain Lewis probably saw the Rocky Mountains.
3. The expedition members were feeling weak and tired.

Page 78
1. The pioneers generally traveled west.
2. The journey from Independence to Portland was about 2,000 miles.
3. Answers will vary but should be at least 100 days. Six months is a more realistic estimate.
4. Answers will vary but should suggest hardships such as disease, hunger, bad weather, harsh living conditions, wild animals, and Native Americans.

Page 79
1. Catherine Pringle means that her father will die soon, that he does not have many days left.
2. Catherine Pringle's father died near Green River.
3. She seems strong and brave.
4.–5. Answers will vary.

Page 80
1. Parkman says he had been without the protection of the law, without a home, and without enough clothes. He had also been hungry and poor.
2. Parkman says that a horse, a rifle, and a knife were his life's necessities. Students' necessities will vary but should be amusing.
3. Parkman means that people had become more primitive. Most of the things of life they had come to expect were not available. They were in the wilderness.
4. Answers will vary but will probably suggest the pioneers had not expected such hardships.
5. Answers will vary.

Page 83
1. The most important thing the Freedmen's Bureau did for the freed slaves was to help them get an education.
2. The Southerners thought that educating the freed slaves would make them more dangerous.
3. Answers will vary.

Page 84
1. For many of the freed slaves, farming was their only skill. The farmland would also give them a place of their own.
2. The white people might cause trouble or try to harm the freed slaves.

Page 85
1. If the freed slaves were citizens, they would get the same rights as all other citizens.
2. Equal protection means that all people are treated the same according to the law.
3. Answers will vary but should suggest that due process keeps people from being thrown in jail for no reason.

Page 86
1. The white men are threatening the freed slave with a gun. White men tried to scare the new African American voters.
2. Answers will vary.

Page 87
1. The Fourteenth Amendment gives all citizens equal protection of the laws.
2. The purpose of most of these actions by Congress was to make life better for the freed slaves and help them adjust.
3. Answers will vary but should directly identify one of the Congressional actions in the chart.
4. Answers will vary but should directly discuss one of the three amendments in the chart.

Page 88
1. The Freedmen's Bureau was abolished in 1872.
2. Corruption in the federal government and financial troubles lowered interest in Reconstruction.
3. The people of the United States seemed

unsatisfied with Republican leadership, so they voted many Democrats into office. Many of those Democrats could have been Southerners just being allowed to vote again.

Page 91
1. Answers will vary but should suggest Lazarus meant that the immigrants wanted to live freely.
2. Answers will vary but should suggest Lazarus meant the golden door was an opening to a new opportunity.
3. Answers will vary but should suggest that the United States is known as the land of opportunity. The immigrants wanted to better their lives.
4. Answers will vary.

Page 92
1. Employment was a major reason immigrants came to the United States in the 1800s.
2. Big cities, such as New York City, were probably common places for immigrants looking for employment to settle.
3. Answers will vary.

Page 93
1. Between 1892 and 1924, 20,003,041 immigrants entered the United States.
2. The most immigrants entered through New York in 1907.
3. The majority of the immigrants entered the United States through New York,

making it important to immigration.

Page 94
1. Life was hard for many new immigrants, and they often had to live crowded together in tenements.
2. Answers will vary but will probably suggest the immigrants did not expect such bad conditions.

Page 95
1. The immigrants went to the libraries to get books to learn.
2. A poor immigrant might never have had a book, so a book might be a precious thing to that person.
3. Libraries gave the immigrants the opportunity to learn about many things and to educate themselves and their children.

Page 98
1. Every group in society was affected by the Great Depression.
2. Many people lost their jobs and their homes.
3. A nomad is a person who wanders. The "nomads of the Depression" were homeless people who wandered around.

Page 99
1. Ben Isaacs's family lost everything when the Great Depression began.
2. First he tried to collect money owed him; then he sold his car for $15; then he went on relief.

Page 100
1. Two effects of the Great Depression were that the gross national product dropped significantly and many people lost their jobs.
2. Answers will vary but should suggest that Hoover did not have a good understanding of the severity of the Great Depression. After he stated the Depression was over, conditions only got worse.

Page 101
1. Roosevelt stated that the value of money and goods has shrunk, taxes have increased, people cannot pay their bills, government has much less money to operate, manufacturing has decreased, farmers cannot sell their crops, people have lost years of savings, and many people must struggle simply to exist on a daily basis.
2. Roosevelt says the nation's main task is to put people to work.
3. The government jobs were meant to complete needed projects and to reorganize the use of natural resources.

Page 102
1. The most people were unemployed in 1933, with 24.9 percent of the labor force without a job.
2. Unemployment decreased because of President Roosevelt's

programs, making them successful.

Page 105
1. west
2. Highway 30; the Oregon Trail
3. Highway 66
4. According to this map, students should name one of the following states: Texas, New Mexico, Oklahoma, Kansas, Colorado, Wyoming, Nebraska, or South Dakota.

Page 106
1. Pay was 35 cents for picking 100 pounds of cotton.
2. Most of the hitchhikers were tenant farmers who had lost everything in the slump in wheat and cotton.
3. Overproduction and underconsumption caused the Oklahoma farmers to be unable to pay their mortgages.

Page 107
1. Most modern highways are concrete or asphalt, and they are often four lanes wide or more. Route 66 appears to be a two-lane, dirt or gravel highway.
2. This family did not appear to have many possessions because everything they had was packed on top of the car and on a small trailer.
3. The pioneers in the 1800s packed everything they had on covered wagons and headed west.
4. Highway 30 followed a route similar to the Oregon Trail.
5. Answers will vary.

Page 110

1. Roosevelt asked Congress to declare war against Japan because Japan had attacked Pearl Harbor.
2. Infamy means dishonor, so December 7, 1941, would be remembered for the dishonorable Japanese attack.
3. Answers will vary.

Page 111

1. Adolf Hitler became the dictator of Germany in 1933.
2. Japan attacked Pearl Harbor, Hawaii, on December 7, 1941.
3. June 6, 1944, became known as D-Day.
4. Germany and Japan surrendered in 1945 to end World War II.

Page 112

1. Germany and Italy
2. In 1941, the Axis forces seemed to be winning the war because they had occupied much of Europe and North Africa.
3. Students should circle one of the neutral countries and give a reasonable response to the question.

Page 113

1. in Hawaii in the Pacific Ocean
2. Students should name one of the following: Guam, Iwo Jima, Philippines, Hawaii.
3. Hiroshima and Nagasaki
4. Answers will vary but might suggest that the United States mainland is a long way from Japan.

Page 114

1. Santa is delivering war bonds as gifts.
2. Answers will vary but may suggest Santa is wearing a helmet to show support for the troops or the war effort.
3. Answers will vary but may suggest that war bonds can help win freedom.

Page 115

1. Women in the United States entered the workplace because many of the men had gone to war overseas.
2. The woman is showing her muscle to demonstrate her strength in the face of adversity.
3. Answers will vary but may suggest that women were supporting their men and the nation.

Page 116

Answers will vary.